IN HIS

Presented to :-

Susan Somerfield

by St. Andrew's Church
on the occasion of
her Confirmation,

1st. April 1981.

IN HIS NAME

PRAYERS FOR THE WORLD
AND THE CHURCH

*A discipline of intercession
based on biblical insights
prepared by*

GEORGE APPLETON

LUTTERWORTH PRESS
Guildford and London

First published 1956

Revised edition first published 1978

ISBN 0 7188 2314 1

Printed in Great Britain by
Fletcher & Son Ltd, Norwich

FOREWORD
TO THE FIRST EDITION

For some years I have felt the need of a discipline of missionary intercession which would help me to pray for the work of the whole Church, and not just that of the Church to which I belong or the missionary society through which I take my share in the Church's mission. I also hoped for a scheme of prayer which would not present missionary intercession as a specialized and separate activity but something integrated in the full range of Christian faith and worship. When the Conference of the International Missionary Council held at Willingen in Germany during July 1952 expressed a need similar to my own, I felt encouraged to make some suggestions to the secretaries of the Council, who responded by asking me to try to meet our mutual need.

The secretaries of the British Council of Churches and my fellow secretaries in the Conference of British Missionary Societies were equally encouraging, expressing the need of some cycle of intercession to deepen the new covenant in Mission and Unity to which these two bodies have set their seal.

The result is this book of prayers and biddings, with the Scriptural insights which inspired them. It is not meant to rival or displace cycles of prayer used by Churches and missionary societies, but to be the wider and more general context in which their particular intercessions can be set.

When I speak of the Church, it includes for me all the Churches of Christendom, including the great Roman Catholic Church and the Ancient Churches of the East as well as the great reformed Churches of the West, and I have dared to pray only that the Church may be what Christ wills it to be.

Many friends have helped with this book of prayers for the World and the Church, and they will recognize the help that they have given, and share in any good effect that our joint effort may produce. Their hope and mine is that Christians in many lands may be awakened to pray with loving and persistent urgency for the world of men for whom Christ died, and for the Church which is the agent of His loving purpose.

G. A.

London, 1955

FOREWORD
TO THE REVISED EDITION

The first edition of *In His Name*, published in 1956, was planned to stimulate a loving concern for the world and the mission of the Church. Many requests have been made for a fourth reprinting, and I am grateful to the Lutterworth Press for being ready to undertake this. In the intervening twenty years there have been two significant developments in the religious life of the world. The first is the revival of other world faiths and the growing recognition that God has never left himself without witness and has been at work always and everywhere to bring people to his truth and salvation. The second is a widespread desire for a deeper spiritual life, shown in the interest in varying methods of prayer and meditation. The revised edition of *In His Name* takes note of these developments and tries to relate intercession to them. In each daily section a devotional thought has been included, which calls for a quiet contemplative approach in which the person praying opens his or her own being to God and is led into receptive, creative and joyful communion with him, so that each of us may become a more deeply worshipping child of God, a more loving disciple of Jesus Christ, a more ready recipient of the graces of the Holy Spirit, and a universal brother or sister to everyone with whom we are brought into contact or of whose needs we become conscious.

G. A.

Wantage, 1978

ACKNOWLEDGEMENTS

Thanks are due to the following publishers, copyright owners and authors (as at 1956) for permission to use prayers (detailed on pp. 195–9) from the undermentioned sources:

British Broadcasting Corporation, *New Every Morning*. Messrs. Burns, Oates & Washbourne, Ltd., *The Life that is Light*. *Christian News-Letter*. Church of Scotland Prayer Union, *The Holy Tryst* (*1940–41*). Edinburgh House Press, *African Ideas of God*. The Epworth Press, *The Book of Offices*. Messrs. Harper Bros., *The World at One in Prayer*. Messrs. Longmans, Green & Co. Ltd., *Cambridge Bede Book; Meditations and Prayers; Per Christum Vinces; Prayers of Citizenship; The Splendour of God*. Messrs. A. R. Mowbray & Co., Ltd., *After the Third Collect; The Church in Germany in Prayer; The Prayer Manual; The Muslim World*. Oxford University Press, *Book of Common Order of the Church of Scotland*, extracts used by permission of the Committee of Public Worship and Aids to Devotion; *Daily Prayer; A Diary of Private Prayer; The Kingdom, the Power and the Glory*. Society for Promoting Christian Knowledge, *Acts of Devotion; A Book of Prayers for Use in an Indian College; My God My Glory; A Procession of Passion Prayers; A War Primer*; and with The Holy Cross Press (U.S.A.), *With Christ in God*. Society for the Propagation of the Gospel, *Prayers of the World-Wide Church*. Student Christian Movement Press, Ltd., *A Devotional Diary; A Book of Prayers for Schools; Prayers in Time of War; Prayers New and Old*. Toc H Incorporated, *A Pocketful of Prayers; A Treasury of Prayers. United Church Observer* (Canada). Universities' Mission to Central Africa, *Prayers for Common Use*. World Dominion Press, *World Dominion, January 1934*. Church Missionary Society; Church Missions to Jews; Industrial Christian Fellowship; Oxford Mission to Calcutta; Society of St. John the Evangelist; the Bishop of Chichester; the Bishop of Sheffield; the Executors of the late Canon Anson, and of

Dean Armitage Robinson; the Rev. W. O. Fitch, S.S.J.E.; the Headmaster of Uppingham School; Mrs. F. B. Macnutt; the Principal, Cuddesdon College; the Very Rev. E. Milner-White; the Rev. John R. G. Ragg; Mrs. William Temple; Mrs. Niebuhr; Bishop John Taylor; the Sisters of the Love of God.

The text of the *Book of Common Prayer* is Crown Copyright and the extracts from this are reproduced by permission. Some lines from the *Prayer Book as Proposed in 1928* have been printed with the permission of the holders of the copyright.

It will be noted that in the scripture extracts which are set at the beginning of each section the Revised Standard Version (1952) of the Bible is used, unless otherwise stated. Gratitude is expressed to the Division of Christian Education of the National Council of the Churches of Christ in the United States of America, and to Messrs. Thomas Nelson & Sons, for permission to make use of these extracts.

If the Compiler has inadvertently infringed any copyright, sincere apologies are offered; any omission will be rectified in future editions.

CONTENTS

WHEN YOU PRAY

Our Father
>God and Father of Jesus Christ,
>>whom we know only through thy Son;
>
>Father of all who have been made thy sons—
>>calling all men to be thy children;
>
>Our Father.

Who art in heaven
>Thou art from everlasting.
>In thee all things exist.
>>Highest and holiest,
>>eternal and perfect.
>
>To thee we lift our spirits
>who art in heaven.

Hallowed be thy name
>May all men know thee as thou art,
>>lifting their hearts to thee
>>in reverence and love.
>
>May every tongue confess thy name,
>>for in thy name
>>will men find salvation.
>
>Hallowed be thy name on earth as it is in heaven.

Thy kingdom come
>King in our hearts;
>Lord of our lives:
>>bringing every thought
>>into captive obedience.
>
>In our own country,
>in every country,
>>the laws of thy kingdom
>>accepted and obeyed.
>
>Thy kingdom come on earth, as it is in heaven.

I

Thy will be done
> Thy wise and loving will
> > in which is our peace.
> > Victory over evil,
> > victory over self,
> > the banishment of war.
> > Men loving in brotherhood
> > > as children of thine
> > > > serving each other.
> Thy will be done on earth as it is in heaven.

Give us this day our daily bread
> Fill us with active pity
> > for the millions who hunger,
> > for the homeless and displaced
> > > who live without hope,
> > for the sick and suffering
> > > whom thou wouldest heal.
> Food too for the soul,
> > the bread of life
> > without which men faint,
> > hungering for thee.
> Give all this day their daily bread.

Forgive us our sins
> Our open crying sins,
> > our secret, whispering sins
> > > which thou alone dost know.
> > Our lack of love,
> > our falling short of thy glory;
> forgive, as we forgive.
> Forgive the selfishness
> > entwined with our nature;
> > the lack of care for others:
> > > 'Am I my brother's keeper?'
> > Our failure to tell good news,
> > > to bring men home to thee.

Teach us to hate the cruelty of men,
    all lust of power,
    all pride of race,
    all greed of gain,
    sin against the truth,
    resentment and revenge.
Forgive us our sins.

Help us to understand the need of others,
    the wrongs they suffer,
    their need of thy forgiveness.
Forgive them and us.

And lead us not into temptation
    Let us not fall back into weakness and sin,
        nor grasp anything which is not thy will.
    Let us not rest content
        or helpless in face of need,
        cowardly in act or speech
        when called to witness
        that we belong to thee.

Deliver us from evil
    Not overcome by evil
        but answering with good,
        with hope and courage high,
        founded in thee.
    More than conquerors
        through him that loved us.
    Enduring to the end
        as seeing thee, our Lord.

For thine is the kingdom,
the power and the glory, for ever and ever.
So let it be. Amen, Amen.

I. GOD OF ALL

1. In the beginning God

In the beginning God created the heavens and the earth . . .
Then God said,
> Let us make man in our image, after our likeness; and let
> them have dominion over the fish of the sea, and over the
> birds of the air, and over the cattle, and over all the earth,
> and over every creeping thing that creeps upon the earth

And God saw everything that he had made, and, behold, it
was very good. *Genesis 1 : 1, 26, 31*

Who has performed and done this, calling the generations
> from the beginning?
> I, the Lord, the first, and with the last; I am he . . .
Before me no god was formed, nor shall there be any after
> me.
I, I am the Lord, and besides me there is no saviour.
Isaiah 41 : 4; 43 : 10, 11

I am the Alpha and the Omega,
> the beginning and the ending,
> says the Lord God,
who is and who was and who is to come, the Almighty.
Revelation 1 : 8

And the Lord will become king over all the earth; on that
> day the Lord will be one and his name one.
Zechariah 14 : 9

4

Let us worship God the Creator

1.   WORTHY ART THOU, our Lord and our God,
        to receive the glory and the honour
            and the power:
        for thou didst create all things,
            and because of thy will
        they were, and were created.

praising him for his eternity

2.   THOU, LORD, in the beginning
            hast laid the foundation of the earth,
            and the heavens are the works
                of thy hands:
        they shall perish; but thou continuest:
        and they all shall wax old
            as doth a garment;
        and as a mantle shalt thou roll them up,
            as a garment,
            and they shall be changed:
        but thou art the same,
        and thy years shall not fail.

praising him for his love of men

3.   FOR THOU LOVEST all the things that are
            and abhorrest nothing which thou hast made:
        for never wouldest thou have made any thing
            if thou hadst hated it.
        And how could anything have endured,
        if it had not been thy will?
        or been preserved, if not called by thee?
      But thou sparest all: for they are thine,
        O Lord, thou lover of souls.

Let us pray

    for all whose horizons are limited by space, matter and
      time;
    for all who, in an age of science, find faith in God difficult;
    for a deeper understanding of the insights of others
      into the beginning of life and the names they give to the

Ultimate-Supreme-Eternal;
for ourselves, lest our own shrunken ideas of God, or our
failure to live as children of God, should hinder men
from coming to him.

4. ALMIGHTY GOD, whose glory the heavens are telling,
the earth thy power, and the sea thy might,
and whose greatness
all feeling and thinking creatures everywhere herald:
To thee belongeth
glory, honour, might, greatness and magnificence,
now and for ever, to the age of ages.

5. O ALMIGHTY GOD, without beginning and without end,
the Lord of thine own works:
We praise and bless thee that thou gavest
a beginning to time,
and to the world in time,
and to mankind in the world;
and we beseech thee so to dispose all men
and all things
that they may be gathered up in thee
and thine endless heaven;
through him who is the first and the last,
thine everlasting Word, our Saviour Jesus Christ.

Beyond words

Thought and words have meditated on the wonder and
beauty of God in creation. Let that insight rest in the
heart, the centre of our being. In the beginning God—
always God—God . . . God . . . God!

6. WORTHY OF PRAISE from every mouth,
of confession from every tongue,
of worship from every creature,
is thy glorious name, O Father, Son and Holy Spirit:
who didst create the world in thy grace
and by thy compassion didst save the world.

2. God with Men

In the beginning was the Word, and the Word was with
    God, and the Word was God . . .
And the Word became flesh and dwelt among us, full of
    grace and truth; we have beheld his glory, glory as of
    the only Son from the Father . . .
No one has ever seen God: the only Son, who is in the bosom
    of the Father, he has made him known.

John 1 : 1, 14, 18

All this took place to fulfil what the Lord had spoken by the
    prophet:
Behold, a virgin shall conceive and bear a son, and his name
    shall be called Emmanuel (which means, God with us).

Matthew 1 : 22, 23

Behold, I stand at the door and knock: if any one hears my
    voice and opens the door, I will come in to him and eat
    with him and he with me.   *Revelation 3 : 20*

Acts of Praise

7.   BLESSED BE THE LORD GOD OF ISRAEL:
    for he hath visited and redeemed his people;
    and hath raised up a mighty salvation for us
        in the house of his servant David.

8.   GLORY BE TO GOD on high,
    and in earth peace, good will towards men.
      We praise thee, we bless thee,
      we worship thee, we glorify thee,
    we give thanks to thee for thy great glory,
      O Lord God, heavenly king,
      God the Father Almighty.

9. HONOUR AND POWER ETERNAL be to thee, O God:
     King of kings and Lord of lords,
        who alone hast immortality,
        dwelling in light unapproachable,
     whom no man has seen, nor can see;
        and to thine only-begotten Son,
        who for us men and for our salvation
        came down from heaven, and was made man,
     and through his death and resurrection
        brought us life and immortality.

Let us pray

10. O GOD OUR FATHER,
     who didst ever receive the upright in heart
        to dwell with thee, as men with God;
        and of thy great love hast deigned,
           in Jesus Christ thy Son,
        to dwell as man with men:
     Make us worthy, we beseech thee,
        both to become thy guests,
        and to receive thee as ours;
     through the same Jesus Christ our Lord.

11. O FATHER, who hast declared thy love to men
     by the birth of the holy child at Bethlehem:
        Help us to welcome him with gladness
     and to make room for him in our common days:
     so that we may live at peace with one another
     and in goodwill with all the family of mankind.

With our Hindu fellow men

12. Lead us from the unreal to the real
     lead us from darkness to light
     lead us from death to immortality.

8

13. ALMIGHTY GOD,
    who didst wonderfully create man in thine own image,
        and didst yet more wonderfully restore him:
    Grant, we beseech thee, that as thy Son
        our Lord Jesus Christ
        was made in the likeness of men,
        so we may be made partakers
            of the divine nature;
    through the same thy Son, Jesus Christ our Lord.

Let the heart rejoice
    in the assurance that God comes to all and to me in Christ.
        Welcome—welcome—welcome!

14. GOD, who didst show forth thy glory in Jesus Christ
        thy Son:
        Grant us so to live in him
            and he in us
        that our lives may reflect thy glory. *Amen.*

3. God in Men

Christ's promise of the Holy Spirit
> And I will pray the Father, and he will give you another
> Counsellor, to be with you for ever, even the Spirit of
> truth, whom the world cannot receive, because it
> neither sees him nor knows him; you know him, for he
> dwells with you, and will be in you.
> I will not leave you desolate; I will come to you . . .
> If a man loves me, he will keep my word, and my Father
> will love him, and we will come to him and make our
> home with him.

John 14 : 16–18, 23

Available for all
> And it shall come to pass afterward, that I will
> > pour out my spirit on all flesh;
> > your sons and your daughters shall prophesy,
> > your old men shall dream dreams,
> and your young men shall see visions.
> > Even upon the menservants and maidservants
> in those days, I will pour out my spirit.

Joel 2 : 28–29

Fulfilment of the promise
> When the day of Pentecost had come,
> they were all together in one place.
> > And suddenly a sound came from heaven
> > > like the rush of a mighty wind, and it filled all
> > > the house where they were sitting.
> > And there appeared to them tongues as of fire,
> > > distributed and resting on each one of them.
> > And they were all filled with the Holy Spirit.

Acts 2 : 1–4

15. TO THEE, O CHRIST, O king exalted,
          we offer up our due praise
          and unfeigned hearty thanks
     for that thou hast sent down and dispersed abroad
          thine own Holy Spirit
     to restore and renew the spirit of men,
     to be the first dedication of thy catholic church on
          earth
     and the first publishing of the gospel to all lands,
          the bond of unity,
          and giver of light and life;
          to whom with the Father and thee,
          one blessed Trinity,
     be ascribed all might, majesty, dominion, and praise,
          now and for ever.

16. O GOD, THE HOLY SPIRIT,
     come to us, and among us:
       come as the wind, and cleanse us;
       come as the fire, and burn;
       come as the dew, and refresh:
     convict, convert, and consecrate
       many hearts and lives
          to our great good
       and thy greater glory,
     and this we ask for Jesus Christ's sake.

17. O HOLY SPIRIT,
          giver of light and life,
     impart to us thoughts higher than our own thoughts,
          and prayers better than our own prayers,
          and powers beyond our own powers,
       that we may spend and be spent
       in the ways of love and goodness,
          after the perfect image
       of our Lord and Saviour Jesus Christ.

Let us pray for all who hold animist beliefs
18. O God, we pray thee for our fellow men
who believe the world of nature
to be indwelt by spirits,
who see in the life of the spring
and the tree
and the fertility of the soil
the action of spiritual beings.
Grant that they may come to know thee
as the Spirit of holiness and love,
and be delivered from all fear,
to worship thee
with the love and reverence of sons,
through Jesus Christ our Lord.

God within
God is in my heart, at the centre of my being. What peace
and joy!
My heart can rest in love and enjoy his presence.

19. Now the God of hope fill us
with all joy and peace in believing,
that we may abound in hope
in the power of the Holy Spirit. *Amen.*

4. God Himself

The unity of God
> Hear, O Israel: The Lord our God is one Lord,
>> and you shall love the Lord your God with all your
>> heart, and with all your
>> soul, and with all your might.

Deuteronomy 6 : 4–5

The three-fold experience
> Go therefore and make disciples of all nations,
>> baptizing them in the name of the Father
>>> and of the Son and of the Holy Spirit,
>> teaching them to observe
>>> all that I have commanded you;
>> and lo, I am with you always,
>>> to the close of the age.

Matthew 28 : 19–20

The three-fold grace
> The grace of the Lord Jesus Christ
>> and the love of God
>> and the fellowship of the Holy Spirit
> be with you all.

2 Corinthians 13 : 14

Let us worship God for revealing the mystery of his being
20.   HOLY ART THOU, O GOD, the Father, who hast made of
        one blood
            all nations of the earth:
      Holy art thou, O God the Son, who hast redeemed all
        mankind
            from the power of darkness:

13

Holy are thou, O God the Holy Spirit, giver of life and
    light,
  by whom the whole church is governed and
    sanctified:
Holy art thou, O God the eternal and adorable Trinity,
  for whose glory man and all created things are,
    and were created:
Glory be to the Father, and to the Son, and to the Holy
    Spirit:
  as it was in the beginning, is now, and ever shall be,
    world without end.

21. WE PRAISE THEE, O GOD,
    we acknowledge thee to be the Lord.
    All the earth doth worship thee,
    the Father everlasting.
  To thee all angels cry aloud,
    the heavens, and all the powers therein.
    To thee cherubin, and seraphin
    continually do cry,

  Holy, Holy, Holy; Lord God of hosts;
  Heaven and earth are full of the majesty of thy glory.

Let us pray
22. BLESS US, O GOD, Father, Son, and Holy Spirit,
    with the vision of thy glory;
    that we may know thee as the Father
    who created us,
    rejoice in thee as the Son who redeemed us,
    and be strong in thee, the Holy Spirit,
    who dost sanctify us;
  keep us steadfast in this faith,
  and bring us at the last
    into thine eternal kingdom,
    where thou art ever worshipped and glorified,
    one God, world without end.

23. O GOD who art eternal and perfect,
        our minds reach upward to know thee.
     Grant us a true spirit of worship
             that gazes in wonder
        at the richness of thy personality and love.
     Help us to experience thee
        as Father, Son and Holy Spirit
     and to worship thee as one God—
        Creator, Saviour and Sanctifier,
     to whom be all glory and praise in earth and heaven,
        both now and to all eternity.

For our Muslim fellow men
24. O LORD JESUS CHRIST, eternal God,
        who didst send forth thy apostles
             in the three-fold name
        to preach the gospel to every creature:
     We pray thee for Muslims in every land.
     We thank thee for their faithfulness
        to the divine unity and majesty,
     and we pray that by the wisdom of thy Spirit
     we and they may be brought to know
        the eternal relationship of love
             within the Godhead,
             and worship thee,
        one God only, blessed for evermore.

Reached by love
     O thou, who cannot be reached by thought and words,
        only by love,
     O my God, I desire to love thee with all my being.

25. BLESSING and honour, and thanksgiving and praise,
             more than we can utter,
             more than we can conceive,
        be unto thee, O holy and glorious Trinity,
             Father, Son, and Holy Spirit,
        by all angels, all men, all creatures,
             for ever and ever. *Amen.*

5. The God of History

All nations, great and small, are destined to be God's people
In that day there will be a highway from Egypt to
Assyria, and the Assyrian will come into Egypt, and the
Egyptian into Assyria, and the Egyptians will worship
with the Assyrians. In that day Israel will be the third
with Egypt and Assyria, a blessing in the midst of the
earth, whom the Lord of hosts has blessed, saying,
Blessed be Egypt my people, and Assyria the work
of my hands, and Israel my heritage.

Isaiah 19 : 23–25

All history before Christ was a preparation for his coming
When the time had fully come, God sent forth his Son,
born of woman, born under the law.

Galatians 4 : 4

The divine plan, known in heaven, is being worked out on earth
The kingdom of the world has become the kingdom of our
Lord and of his Christ, and he shall reign for ever and
ever ... King of kings and Lord of lords.

Revelation 11 : 15; 19 : 16

Let us praise God
for his activity in creation, in history, through Israel,
supremely through the incarnation of Jesus Christ,
and in the working of the Holy Spirit;
for the revelation of God's purpose and righteousness in
history;
for his activity in other faiths, inspiring all that is true,
righteous and loving;
for the expression of his love to the uttermost in the cross of
Jesus Christ.

16

26.   Grant us to look with thine eyes of compassion,
O merciful God, at the long travail of mankind:
the wars, the hungry millions,
the countless refugees,
the natural disasters,
the cruel and needless deaths,
men's inhumanity to one another,
the heartbreak and hopelessness of so many lives.
Hasten the coming of the messianic age
when the nations shall be at peace,
and men shall live free from fear and free from want
and there shall be no more pain or tears,
in the security of thy will
and the assurance of thy love,
shown us in Jesus the Christ, the Saviour of all.

27.   ALL THY WORKS praise thee, O Lord,
and thy saints give thanks unto thee.
They show the glory of thy kingdom
and talk of thy power;
that thy power, thy glory,
and mightiness of thy kingdom
might be known unto men.
Thy kingdom is an everlasting kingdom
and thy dominion endureth throughout all ages.

28.   THY KINGDOM COME,
in the assurance to all nations of their right to life
and freedom,
in the deliverance of mankind from the slavery of
armaments,
in the establishment of the reign of law between
nations,
in the recognition of the rights of minorities,
in the right use of the resources of the earth,
in the rekindling of a passion for truth,
in the opening of springs of mercy and compassion:
thy reign over every thought, affection and impulse of
our being.

Eternal will and eternal patience, working out the purpose
of eternal love.

Let my heart be silent before thee, in wonder.

29. To HIM who sits upon the throne and to the Lamb,
be blessing and honour and glory and might,
for ever and ever. *Amen.*

6. The First People of God

God's call to Abraham
Now the Lord said to Abram, Go from your country and
your kindred and your father's house to the land that I
will show you. And I will make of you a great nation, and
I will bless you, and make your name great, so that you
will be a blessing ... and by you all the families of the
earth will bless themselves.   *Genesis 12 : 1, 2, 3*

His covenant with Israel
Now therefore, if you will obey my voice and keep my
covenant, you shall be my own possession among all
peoples; for all the earth is mine, and you shall be to me
a kingdom of priests and a holy nation.   *Exodus 19 : 5–6*

Israel is to spread true religion over all the earth
And now the Lord says: It is too light a thing that you
should be my servant to raise up the tribes of Jacob and
to restore the preserved of Israel; I will give you as a
light to the nations, that my salvation may reach to the
end of the earth.   *Isaiah 49 : 6*

Their inclusion will bring even greater blessing
Now if their trespass means riches for the world, and if
their failure means riches for the Gentiles, how much
more will their full inclusion mean! ... For if their
rejection means the reconciliation of the world, what
will their acceptance mean but life from the dead?

Romans 11 : 12, 15

Let us thank God
for his call of one man
through whom all nations are to be blessed;

19

for his call of one nation
    through whom all nations shall be brought to him;
for the one Lord and Saviour
    born of Jewish race and available for Jew
    and Gentile alike;
for the growth of a new spirit
    of understanding and friendship between
    Christians and Jews, both claiming to
    be children of Abraham and the people of God.

Let us offer our penitence to God
    for the injustice done to the Jewish people all
    down through the centuries;
    for the church's responsibility in the past for the
    persecution of the Jewish people;
    for its wholesale accusation of the Jews for
    the murder of Jesus;
    for its failure to show the love of Jesus in all
    relations with his people;
    for its refusal to see continuing validity and effectiveness
    in Judaism.

30. O Lord, who hast chosen to thyself a special people,
        Israel,
        through whom thy way might be known upon earth,
        thy saving health among all nations:
    Grant that we and all those who once were far off,
        but now have been made nigh by the blood of Christ,
        may with clearer eyes behold
        thy steadfast purpose for thy chosen people
    manifested in Jesus Christ our Lord.

31. O Lord, who didst send forth thine apostles everywhere
        preaching the word,
        look upon thine ancient people still scattered abroad:
        send to them the light of thy gospel,
            and hasten the time
        when thou, Lord Jesus, shalt become
        the glory of thy people Israel.

32.   O LORD, we beseech thee, let thy continual pity
        cleanse and defend thy church;
    and, because it cannot continue in safety
        without thy succour,
    preserve it evermore by thy help and goodness;
        through Jesus Christ our Lord.

33.   O GOD, who didst choose for thyself a nation
        to be thy agent in the world
        and didst enlarge it
        in the church of thy Son:
  Grant that thy church may be truly the body of
        Christ,
      giving itself for the world
        as thou didst give thy Son
        and as he did give his life.
  Let thy church be a light to the nations,
      the messenger of thy gospel,
      the agent of thy salvation.
  And to us who are members of thy body,
  give faithfulness, obedience, zeal and love,
  that thy wise and loving purpose may be
      accomplished
  and all men may know thee as their God and
      Saviour,
      through Jesus Christ our Lord.

Chosen and Choosing

  O God, you call every nation to receive blessing and co-
  operate in your loving purpose. You choose us all.
  May all choose you! We all belong to you, our God as well as
  theirs, their God as well as ours.

34.   BLESSED BE THE LORD GOD, the God of Israel,
      who only doeth wondrous things:
    and blessed be his glorious name for ever;
    and let the whole earth be filled with his glory.
        Amen, and Amen.

7. Israel Enlarged

So you see that it is men of faith who are the
    sons of Abraham . . . So then, those who are men of faith
    are blessed with Abraham who had faith.   *Galatians 3 : 7, 9*

So then you are no longer strangers and sojourners,
    but you are fellow citizens with the saints
        and members of the household of God,
            built upon the foundation
        of the apostles and prophets,
    Christ Jesus himself being the chief cornerstone,
        in whom the whole structure
        is joined together
        and grows into a holy temple in the Lord,
    in whom you also are built into it
    for a dwelling place of God in the Spirit.   *Ephesians 2 : 19–22*

But you are a chosen race,
        a royal priesthood,
        a holy nation,
        God's own people,
    that you may declare the wonderful deeds
    of him who called you out of darkness
        into his marvellous light.
    Once you were no people
        but now you are God's people;
    once you had not received mercy
        but now you have received mercy.   *1 Peter 2 : 9, 10*

Meditation
    Let us meditate on the church universal,
        the enlarged people of God,
        the community through whom God wills to bless
        and save all nations.

Let us remember how, inspired by the Holy Spirit,
 it spread to the ends of the earth,
 proclaiming what God had done in Christ
 and calling men to accept his salvation.

Let us thank God for its faithfulness in facing persecution,
 for the Holy Spirit's protection in times of weakness
  and darkness,
 for the inner band who maintained the flame of faith
  and devotion when times were difficult.

Let us recall the medieval missionaries who brought the
  pagan tribes of the west to Christ,
 and the great missionary movements of the last 150 years,
 through which new churches have been brought
  into being
 and are now taking their part in God's eternal
  purpose of blessing.
Let us pray for the guidance of God in the church's encounter
 with the religions of mankind.

Let us pray

35. O GOD, mighty to save, infinite in compassion towards
the nations that know thee not, and the tongues
which cannot speak thy name: We humbly thank
thee that thou hast made the church of thy dear Son
the chariot of the gospel, to tell it out among the
nations that thou art king, and to bear thy love unto
the world's end; and for all thy servants who counted
not their lives dear unto them on this employment,
and for all peoples newly praising thee, we praise
and bless thee, Father, Son and Holy Spirit, one
Lord and God for ever and ever.

36. O GOD, we pray thee for thy church
 which is set today amid the perplexities
  of a changing order,
 and is face to face with a new task.
Fill us all afresh with the Spirit of Pentecost.

Help us to proclaim boldly the coming of thy kingdom.
    And do thou hasten the time
when the knowledge of thyself shall fill the earth
    as the waters cover the sea.

37. BLESS all work in thy field: Bless thy messengers:
    Bless the seed of thy word
        and grant that it bring forth fruit.
    Bless all who are joined in thee:
    Bless thy church.
Thou buildest thy kingdom amongst us.
Thou buildest thy kingdom in all the world.

38. ALMIGHTY AND EVERLASTING GOD, by whose Spirit the
whole body of the church is governed and sanctified:
Receive our prayers, which we offer before thee for
all members of thy holy church, that every member
in his vocation and ministry may truly and godly
serve thee; through our Lord and Saviour Jesus
Christ.

Let every heart rejoice
    Dear God, you burst our narrow bonds. We cannot
    confine you, monopolize you, control you. Out beyond
    Israel, beyond the church, beyond the religions, to the
    ends of the universe, embracing every creature, O God!

39. THOU ART WORTHY, O LORD, to receive power,
        and riches,
           and wisdom, and strength,
       and honour, and glory, and blessing.
For the light of thy everlasting gospel,
    sent forth to every nation, and kindred,
        and tongue, and people,
    shining so long amongst ourselves:
for thy church, the pillar and ground of the truth,
    against which the gates of hell shall not prevail:
all glory be to thee, O Lord. *Amen.*

II. GOD-MAN

8. Jesus is Lord

The first confession
>
> Now when Jesus came into the district of Caesarea Philippi, he asked his disciples, Who do men say that the Son of man is?
>
> And they said, Some say John the Baptist, others say Elijah, and others Jeremiah or one of the prophets.
>
> He said to them, But who do you say that I am?
>
> Simon Peter replied, You are the Christ, the Son of the living God. *Matthew 16 : 13–16*

The Holy Spirit inspires each confession
>
> Therefore I want you to understand that no one speaking by the Spirit of God ever says Jesus be cursed!
>
> and no one can say Jesus is Lord except by the Holy Spirit.
> *1 Corinthians 12 : 3*

Every tongue shall confess
>
> Therefore God has highly exalted him and bestowed on him the name which is above every name,
>
> that at the name of Jesus every knee should bow, in heaven and on earth and under the earth,
>
> and every tongue confess that Jesus Christ is Lord, to the glory of God the Father. *Philippians 2 : 9–11*

Let us praise God
>
> for the acknowledgement by men and women in all lands that Jesus is Lord;

for the faith of those in village and town who show by their
lives the lordship of Christ;

for those who venture forth into new lands to witness to
Christ as Saviour and Lord;

for those who penetrate into new areas of thought and work
to claim them for the lordship of Christ;

for those who witness to Christ in places where Christians are
a small minority or where witness is costly, dangerous or
liable to be ridiculed;

for the communion of the faithful the world over who
worship and witness together in a non-Christian or post-
Christian environment.

Down in the heart

Let the very thought of Jesus fill the heart with love and
gratitude and devotion.

40. WE BESEECH THEE, LORD JESUS, to enlighten thy people,
and always set their hearts aflame with the fire of thy
glory; that they may ever acknowledge thee as their
Saviour and inwardly behold thee as their Lord, who
with the Father and the Holy Spirit livest and reignest, ever one God, world without end.

41. O LORD, thou art the king of our spirits. Thou hast
issued orders to thy subjects to do a great work. Thou
hast commanded them to preach the gospel to every
creature. We are going on that errand now. Let thy
presence go with us to quicken us and enable us to
persevere in the great work until we die.

42. O CHRIST OUR GOD, in our acts this day,
the words we speak, the thoughts we think,
the fulfilment of our common tasks,
the relationships of our ordinary life,
thy kingdom come, thy will be done,
on earth as it is in heaven.

THE GRACE of our Lord Jesus Christ be with us all. *Amen.*

9. Christ our Example

He opened the book where it was written,
The Spirit of the Lord is upon me, because he has anointed me to preach good news to the poor. He has sent me to proclaim release to the captives and recovering of sight to the blind, to set at liberty those who are oppressed, to proclaim the acceptable year of the Lord.
And he began to say to them, Today this scripture has been fulfilled in your hearing.

Luke 4 : 17–19, 21

Until we all attain to the unity of the faith and of the knowledge of the Son of God, to mature manhood, to the measure of the stature of the fullness of Christ.

Ephesians 4 : 13

For to this you have been called, because Christ also suffered for you, leaving you an example, that you should follow in his steps. He committed no sin; no guile was found on his lips.

1 Peter 2 : 21–22

Meditation
43.   LET HIM BE THY MODEL
          for thy every word and deed,
       moving or standing,
          seated, eating,
          silent or speaking,
          alone or with others.
          Study him
       and thou wilt grow in his love.
          In his company
       thou wilt gain sweetness and confidence
       and thou wilt be strengthened in every virtue.

27

Let this be thy wisdom
   this thy meditation
   this thy study
to have him always in mind
   to move thee to imitation
   to win thee to his love.

Let us pray

44. O LORD JESUS CHRIST,
      who didst deign to be made like unto men:
         the sharer of our sorrows,
         the companion of our journeys,
         the light of our ignorance,
         the remedy of our infirmity:
      So fill us with thy Spirit
         and endue us with thy grace
      that as thou hast been made like unto us,
      we may grow more like unto thee,
         for thy tender mercies' sake.

45. COME, LORD! come with me; see with my eyes; hear
      with my ears; think with my mind; love with my
      heart—in all the situations of my life.
      Work with my hands, my strength. Take, cleanse,
      possess, inhabit my will, my understanding, my love.
      Take me where you will, to do what you want, in your
      way.

Prayer of the heart

   Day by day, dear Lord, I pray three things of you, to
   know you more clearly, love you more dearly, follow
   you more nearly, day by day.

46. MAY THE LOVE of the Lord Jesus
         draw us to himself;
      May the power of the Lord Jesus
         strengthen us in his service;
      May the joy of the Lord Jesus
         fill our souls. *Amen.*

10. The Way

You know the way where I am going.
Lord, we do not know where you are going;
   how can we know the way?
I am the way . . . no one comes to the Father, but by me.
Lord, show us the Father, and we shall be satisfied.
Have I been with you so long, and yet you do not
   know me? He who has seen me has seen the Father.

John 14 : 4–6; 8–9

If any man would come after me, let him deny
   himself and take up his cross and follow me.

Mark 8 : 34

Act of Faith

47.   Lord, I believe that thou art the way, the truth and
the life. Make me so to walk with thee that by thee I
may come to the Father; make my faith strong to
believe all that thou hast revealed, for thou art the
very truth. Give me thy life that I may say, I live, yet
not I, but Christ liveth in me. By thy divine om-
nipotence direct and strengthen my faith; by thy
divine wisdom instruct and enlighten it; by thy
divine goodness sustain and perfect it, that I may
abide in thee, unchanging to the end.

Let us pray

48.   O Almighty God, whom truly to know is everlasting
life: Grant us perfectly to know thy Son Jesus Christ
to be the way, the truth, and the life; that . . . we
may steadfastly walk in the way that leadeth to eternal life; through the same thy Son Jesus Christ our
Lord.

49. MOST LOVING FATHER, who willest us to give thanks for all things, to dread nothing but the loss of thee, and to cast all our care on thee who carest for us; preserve us from faithless fears and worldly anxieties, and grant that no clouds of this mortal life may hide from us the light of that love which is immortal, and which thou hast manifested unto us in thy Son, Jesus Christ our Lord.

50. OUR FATHER, we thank thee that thou hast raised us from sleep. We are indebted to thy patience with us when we fail to do thy will.
    It is known to thee that we are worthless.
    Thou seest our lack of love: forgive us.
    Fill us, our Father, with thy Holy Spirit
        that we may be able to love thee.
    Thine outstretched hand is before us, extending gifts to us. We have not held out ours to receive them. Have mercy on us. Press open our hands and deposit therein thy mercies.
    Thou hast called us to gather, and we do but scatter. Thou hast commanded us to follow thee,
        and we have not risen. Raise us, O God.
    Do not wait for what we shall do:
        go on, O Lord, with thy kindness.
    Make thy name holy in this land
        through the mercy of our Lord Jesus Christ.

Always ahead
    Dear Lord, you are always ahead, beckoning me on to the Father's will. All I have to do is to follow.

51. JESUS, OUR MASTER, do thou meet us while we walk in the way and long to reach the heavenly country; so that, following thy light, we may keep the way of righteousness, and never wander away into the darkness of this world's night, while thou, who art the way, the truth, and the light art shining within us; for thy mercy's sake. *Amen.*

11. The Truth

And the Word became flesh and dwelt among us, full of
    grace and truth;
  we have beheld his glory, glory as of the only Son
    from the Father.

John 1 : 14

In many and various ways God spoke of old to our fathers by
  the prophets; but in these last days he has spoken to us by
  a Son, whom he appointed the heir of all things, through
  whom also he created the world.
He reflects the glory of God and bears the very stamp of his
  nature, upholding the universe by his word of power.

Hebrews 1 : 1–3

Jesus spoke to them, saying,
  I am the light of the world; he who follows me will not
  walk in darkness, but will have the light of life.

John 8 : 12

And we know that the Son of God has come and has given us
    understanding, to know him who is true;
  and we are in him who is true, in his Son Jesus Christ.
This is the true God and eternal life.

1 John 5 : 20

Let us thank God
  for those of many races and nations who have been called
    out of the darkness of superstition and error, and out of
    the twilight of unredeemed religion, into the light of the
    truth of the Christian faith;

31

for the truthfulness and honesty that it demands of us, the
  emptying from the heart of unworthiness of thought and
  intention;

for light from the Bible to uphold and sustain and guide
  us;

for the focusing of vision on the perfection of Jesus Christ,
  true God and true Man;

for the release from bondage into the service of him whose
  service is perfect freedom;

for the infection of the knowledge of the truth that comes
  to us in those about us who have been with Jesus.

Let us pray

52.   O LORD JESUS CHRIST,
          who art the way, the truth, and the life;
              we pray thee
          suffer us not to stray from thee, who art the way,
          nor to distrust thee who art the truth,
          nor to rest in any other thing than thee,
              who art the life.
          Teach us by thy Holy Spirit
              what to believe,
              what to do,
              and wherein to take our rest.
          For thine own name's sake we ask it.

53.   O GOD who art nigh to all them
          that call upon thee in truth;
              who art thyself the truth,
              whom to know is perfect knowledge:
          Instruct us with thy divine wisdom,
              and teach us thy law;
              that we may know the truth and walk in it;
          through him in whom the truth was made manifest,
          even Jesus Christ, thy Son, our Lord.

54. O THOU to whom we always look,
      lighten our hearts
      as the sun throws light
    upon the dark bushes around us.
May we always reflect thy radiance
    so that those who have not known thee
      may see thee in us.
In the name of the great light we ask this.

Truth through Christ
    O Christ, you have shown us that all truth is in God. You
lead us to God, the original and final truth.

55. ALMIGHTY GOD,
who hast sent the Spirit of truth unto us
    to guide us into all truth:
We beseech thee so to rule our lives
    by thy power,
    that we may be truthful
    in word and deed and thought.
O keep us, most merciful Saviour,
    with thy gracious protection,
that no fear or hope may ever make us false
    in act or speech.
Cast out from us whatsoever loveth or maketh a lie;
and bring us all into the perfect freedom
    of thy truth;
through Jesus Christ thy Son our Lord.

MAY ALL THE PEOPLES, from the rising of the sun,
    even unto the going down of the same,
cry aloud in thy praise with joyful voice,
      and say:
    Glory be to thee, O God,
    the Saviour of all,
      for ever and ever. *Amen.*

12. The Life

I came that they may have life, and have it abundantly ...
And this is eternal life, that they know thee the only true
God, and Jesus Christ whom thou hast sent.

John 10 : 10; 17 : 3

Whoever drinks of the water that I shall give him will never
thirst; the water that I shall give him will become in him a
spring of water welling up to eternal life.
He who believes in me, as the scripture has said, Out of his
heart shall flow rivers of living water.

John 4 : 14; 7 : 38

I am the resurrection and the life; he who believes in me,
though he die, yet shall he live, and whoever lives and
believes in me shall never die.

John 11 : 25–26

That which was from the beginning,
   which we have heard,
   which we have seen with our eyes,
   which we have looked upon
   and touched with our hands,
      concerning the word of life—
   the life was made manifest,
   and we saw it,
   and testify to it,
   and proclaim to you the eternal life
      which was with the Father
      and was made manifest to us—
that which we have seen and heard
   we proclaim also to you.

1 John 1 : 1–3

Meditation

In the knowledge of God through Christ,
and our response to that revelation,
is our eternal life.
All spiritual life comes from Christ.
He is the vitalizing energy of all that lives,
the spring of whatever vitality we have.
As we commit ourselves in obedience to Christ,
his life flows into us—
abundant life,
enough for our own deepest needs
and running over for the use of others.
His life in us develops a new kind of life,
which physical death cannot destroy.
If we do not let other people know
of this unfailing source of life,
we fail both in gratitude to Christ
and in love towards our fellow men.

Let us pray

56. ALMIGHTY GOD,
who through thine only-begotten Son Jesus Christ
hast overcome death,
and opened unto us the gate of everlasting life:
We humbly beseech thee,
that as by thy special grace going before us
thou dost put into our minds good desires,
so by thy continual help
we may bring the same to good effect;
through Jesus Christ our Lord,
who liveth and reigneth
with thee and the Holy Spirit,
ever one God, world without end.

57. O LIVING GOD,
in whom is the fountain of life:
So teach us to know thee

through Jesus Christ
that we may share the power
  of that eternal life
  which is in him,
and that all our lives
may be brought into obedience
  to thy holy will;
through the same Jesus Christ our Lord.

58.   O GOD, THE LIVING GOD,
who hast put thine own eternity
    in our hearts,
    and hast made us to hunger and thirst
      after thee:
Satisfy, we pray thee, the instincts
  which thou hast implanted in us,
  that we may find thee in life,
    and life in thee;
  through Jesus Christ our Lord.

Life through Christ
  O God, deep down in the core of my being, you are the
  source of my life, the spring of my vitality.

        MAY THE LORD bless us,
        and preserve us from all evil,
        and keep us in eternal life. *Amen.*

13. Not to destroy, but to fulfil

Christ is the fulfilment
of Israel's hopes
>Think not that I have come to abolish the law
>   and the prophets;
>I have come not to abolish them but to fulfil them.

Matthew 5 : 17

All spiritual light before Christ
came from him
>The true light that enlightens every man was coming into
>   the world.

John 1 : 9

Paul preaching before a
rural pagan congregation, says
>Men, why are you doing this? We also are men, of like
>nature with you, and bring you good news, that you
>should turn from these vain things to a living God who
>made the heaven and the earth and the sea and all that
>is in them. In past generations he allowed all the nations
>to walk in their own ways; yet he did not leave himself
>without witness, for he did good and gave you from
>heaven rains and fruitful seasons, satisfying your hearts
>with food and gladness.

Acts 14 : 15–17

And at Athens he quotes
the witness of pagan writers
>In him we live and move and have our being;
>   as even some of your poets have said,
>For we are indeed his offspring.

Acts 17 : 28

Yet he is definite in his demand
for a new life for Gentile converts

You did not so learn Christ!—assuming that you have
heard about him and were taught in him, as the truth is
in Jesus.

Put off your old nature which belongs to your former
manner of life and is corrupt through deceitful lusts, and
be renewed in the spirit of your minds, and put on the
new nature, created after the likeness of God in true
righteousness and holiness.   *Ephesians 4 : 20–24*

Salvation came through one nation,
that all nations should be blessed

For salvation is from the Jews.   *John 4 : 22*

The Jews are entrusted with the oracles of God . . .

. . . and to them belong the sonship, the glory, the
covenants, the giving of the law, the worship, and the
promises; . . . and of their race, according to the flesh, is
the Christ.   *Romans 3 : 2; 9 : 4, 5*

My heart's desire

O Christ, let me be a recognizer, a fulfiller, a builder with
you of all that is true, good, beautiful and loving.

59.   O GOD, who hast made of one blood
                 all nations of men
               for to dwell on the face of the earth,
         and didst send thy blessed Son Jesus Christ
         to preach peace to them that are afar off,
               and to them that are nigh:
         Grant that all the peoples of the world
         may feel after thee and find thee;
               and hasten, O Lord,
               the fulfilment of thy promise
               to pour out thy Spirit
                 upon all flesh;
               through Jesus Christ our Lord.

60. O ETERNAL WORD,
    who from the beginning hast revealed
    glimpses of truth and righteousness
    through prophets of many faiths,
        we praise thee
    that all that is of value
    is found fulfilled and perfected
        in thee,
    and all that is mistaken
    finds its correction
        in thee.
Do thou draw all seekers of truth and righteousness
        to thyself,
and vouchsafe to them the unsearchable riches
    that can be found in thee.
We rejoice in thy salvation, knowing
    that we have been saved
    in thy blest name
        O Jesus Christ,
        our Saviour and our Lord.

MAY ALL THE NATIONS whom thou hast made
    come and worship thee, O Lord,
        and glorify thy name. *Amen.*

14. Behold, I make all things new

No one sews a piece of unshrunk cloth on an old
    garment; if he does, the patch tears away from it, the
    new from the old, and a worse tear is made.
And no one puts new wine into old wine-skins; if he does, the
    wine will burst the skins, and the wine is lost, and so are
    the skins; but new wine is for fresh skins.

Mark 2 : 21–22

Therefore, if any one is in Christ,
    he is a new creation;
the old has passed away,
    behold, the new has come.

2 Corinthians 5 : 17

Then I saw a new heaven and a new earth;
    for the first heaven and the first earth
        had passed away, and the sea was no more . . .
and I heard a great voice from the throne saying,
    Behold, the dwelling of God is with men.
    He will dwell with them,
    and they shall be his people,
    and God himself will be with them . . .
And he who sat upon the throne said,
    Behold, I make all things new.

Revelation 21 : 1, 3, 5

Meditation
    Christ demands that if we belong to him,
    the whole of our nature must be re-made.
        It is not sufficient to deal with one or two sins
        or to add one or two new duties.
    We must be born again.

Respectable lives,
which avoid scandalous sins
and practise what men may judge generous giving,
    are not enough.
Christ demands conversion,
    the total offering of our souls and bodies,
    all that we are and all that we have,
    and all that we may become by his grace.

Only then can Christ use us
    to make the new world which is his will.
Only then shall we understand
    how constantly he is making all things new,
    creating them in the original pattern
        which God willed for them.

Let us pray

61. O GOD, who sitting on the throne sayest,
            Behold, I make all things new:
        Fulfil now thy work in thy church.
            Instil into it a sense
                of the brotherhood of nations.
            Form them into one great family.
        Let every nation with new devotion
            bring its peculiar gifts,
            and lay them at thy feet,
            to be adornments of thy kingdom;
                that we may see fulfilled
                the saying that is written,
        The kingdom of the world is become
    the kingdom of our Lord and of his Christ.

62. O JESUS CHRIST, who art the same yesterday, today and
        for ever: Pour thy spirit upon the church that it may
        preach thee anew to each succeeding generation.
        Grant that it may interpret the eternal gospel in
        terms relevant to the life of each new age, and as the

41

fulfilment of the highest hopes and the deepest needs
of every nation; so that at all times and in all places
men may see in thee their Lord and Saviour.

63.   I am no longer my own, but thine.
        Put me to what thou wilt,
        rank me with whom thou wilt;
        put me to doing, put me to suffering;
    let me be employed for thee, or laid aside for thee,
        exalted for thee, or brought low for thee;
        let me be full, let me be empty;
        let me have all things, let me have nothing;
    I freely and heartily yield all things
        to thy pleasure and disposal.
    And now, O glorious and blessed God,
        thou art mine, and I am thine. So be it.
    And the covenant which I have made on earth,
        let it be ratified in heaven.

In stillness

I hold myself before you, O God, in stillness, waiting for
    your renewing, sanctifying, inspiring. Still and open
    before you, O God, my God.

MAY THE LORD forgive what we have been;
        sanctify what we are;
        and order what we shall be;
            for his name's sake. *Amen.*

III. SAVIOUR

15. Come unto Me

Hearken to me, O house of Jacob, all the remnant of the house of Israel, who have been borne by me from your birth, carried from the womb;
even to your old age I am he, and to gray hairs I will carry you. I have made, and I will bear; I will carry and will save.   *Isaiah 46 : 3, 4*

Come to me, all who labour and are heavy-laden, and I will give you rest.
Take my yoke upon you, and learn from me; for I am gentle and lowly in heart, and you will find rest for your souls. For my yoke is easy, and my burden is light.

Matthew 11 : 28–30

Apart from me you can do nothing.   *John 15 : 5*

Let us pray
  that men everywhere may hear and receive these promises of a gracious and loving saviour;
  that they may lay at his feet their burdens of sin, sorrow, difficulty, and worry, and may find their rest in him;
  that the church may preach this gospel with courage and love, knowing that Christ can satisfy men's deepest needs.

43

64. O LORD, thou hast made us for thyself,
    and our hearts shall find no rest,
    until they find their rest in thee.

In quietness
I come to you, O gracious Lord, to learn from you, and be
refreshed and renewed.

65. GRANT, we beseech thee, merciful Lord, to thy faithful
    people pardon and peace, that we may be cleansed
    from all our sins, and serve thee with a quiet mind;
    through Jesus Christ our Lord.

66. O LORD GOD, in whom we live, and move, and have
    our being, open our eyes that we may behold thy
    fatherly presence ever about us. Draw our hearts to
    thee with the power of thy love. Teach us to be
    anxious for nothing, and when we have done what
    thou hast given us to do, help us, O God our Saviour,
    to leave the issue to thy wisdom. Take from us all
    doubt and mistrust. Lift our thoughts up to thee in
    heaven, and make us to know that all things are
    possible to us through thy Son, our Redeemer.

67. LET US NOT seek out of thee
    what we can only find in thee, O Lord!
    Peace and rest and joy and bliss,
    which abide only in thine abiding joy.
    Lift up our souls above the weary round of
    harassing thoughts to thy eternal presence.
    Lift up our minds to the pure, bright, serene
    atmosphere of thy presence,
            that we may breathe freely,
            there repose in thy love,
            there be at rest from ourselves
            and from all things that weary us:

and thence return, arrayed in thy peace,
to do and to bear
whatsoever shall best please thee.

GRACE to us and peace be multiplied in the
knowledge of God and of Jesus Christ our Lord.

Amen.

16. The Gospel of Forgiveness

Let us remember the many texts in the New Testament
which proclaim God's full and free forgiveness

My son, your sins are forgiven. *Mark 2 : 5*

Father forgive them; for they know not what they do.

Luke 23 : 34

The saying is sure and worthy of full acceptance, that
Christ Jesus came into the world to save sinners. And I
am the foremost of sinners. *1 Timothy 1 : 15*

But God shows his love for us in that while we were yet
sinners Christ died for us. *Romans 5 : 8*

God was in Christ reconciling the world to himself, not
counting their trespasses against them, and entrusting to
us the message of reconciliation. *2 Corinthians 5 : 19*

If any one does sin, we have an advocate with the Father,
Jesus Christ the righteous; and he is the expiation for
our sins, and not for ours only but also for the sins of the
whole world. *1 John 2 : 1, 2*

So we are ambassadors for Christ, God making his appeal
through us. We beseech you on behalf of Christ, be
reconciled to God. *2 Corinthians 5 : 20*

Let us thank God
for conscience operating in men everywhere,
reminding them of their need of forgiveness;
for God's free gift of forgiveness,
which cannot be earned or won or deserved,
but only accepted simply and trustingly;
that God not only forgives,
but gives us grace to conquer sin;
that he has entrusted us with this good news
that sin can be forgiven.

68. REJOICE over me, O God the Father, that this thy child was lost, but is found; was dead, but is alive again.

Rejoice over me, O God the Son, that thy loud cries and tears and bitter agonies which for my sake thou didst endure upon the cross, were not so unhappily lost, as to be cast away in vain upon me.

Rejoice over me, O God the Holy Spirit, that thy so many secret and powerful touches have at last got the upper hand of me.

Rejoice over me, O ye holy angels, whose ministry it is to rejoice at the conversion of a sinner.

69. O GOD, whose nature and property is ever to have mercy and to forgive, receive our humble petitions; and though we be tied and bound with the chain of our sins, yet let the pitifulness of thy great mercy loose us; for the honour of Jesus Christ, our mediator and advocate.

70. GIVE US, O LORD, a humble spirit, that we may never presume upon thy mercy, but live always as those who have been much forgiven. Make us tender and compassionate toward those who are overtaken by temptation, considering ourselves, how we have fallen in times past and may fall yet again. Make us watchful and sober-minded, looking ever unto thee for grace to stand upright, and to preserve unto the end; through thy Son Jesus Christ our Lord.

The Jesus Prayer

Lord ... Jesus ... Christ ... Son of God ... have mercy ... on me ... a sinner ... forgive ... comfort ... and heal me.

UNTO HIM that loved us, and washed us from our sins, and hath made us kings and priests unto God, and his Father,

unto him be glory and dominion, for ever and ever.

Amen.

17. The Cross of Christ

And I, when I am lifted up from the earth, will draw all men
to myself.   *John 12 : 32*

For God so loved the world that he gave his only Son, that
   whoever believes in him should not perish but have
   eternal life.
For God sent the Son into the world, not to condemn the
   world, but that the world might be saved through him.
                                                       John 3 : 16–17

Why, one will hardly die for a righteous man—though per-
   haps for a good man one will dare even to die.
But God shows his love for us in that while we were yet
   sinners Christ died for us.   *Romans 5 : 7–8*

For I decided to know nothing among you except Jesus
   Christ and him crucified.   *1 Corinthians 2 : 2*

Meditation
   It is the cross of Christ that draws men
      in every country and in every age,
            more than his teaching,
         more than his life of holiness,
         more than his miracles of power and love.
   The cross declares God's love for men;
      God loves men as much as this.
   The cross shows what men's sins do to God;
      sin causes all this pain to God.
   The cross of Christ was a thing which happened historically,
      on a particular day, for all men.
   Only when its significance becomes personal to each
      can we realize its deepest meaning
               and say with Paul,
   The Son of God, who loved me, and gave himself for me.

48

71.   BLESSED BE THY NAME, O JESU,
        Son of the most high God;
    blessed be the sorrow thou sufferedst
      when thy holy hands and feet were nailed
          to the tree;
      and blessed thy love when,
      the fullness of pain accomplished,
    thou didst give thy soul into the hands
        of the Father;
      so by thy cross and precious blood
      redeeming all the world,
      all longing souls departed
      and the numberless unborn;
  who now livest and reignest in the glory
        of the eternal Trinity
        for ever and ever.

72.   O LORD GOD, keep ever in our remembrance
    the life and death of our Saviour Jesus Christ.
      Make the thought of his love powerful
        to win us from evil.
    As he toiled and sorrowed and suffered for us,
      in fighting against sin,
  so may we endure constantly and labour diligently,
    as his soldiers and servants,
      looking ever unto him
      and counting it all joy
    to be partakers with him in his conflict,
      his cross, and his victory;
    through the same Jesus Christ our Lord.

In the cross
    Let me reflect on your love, O Christ, as shining through
      your love we see the love of the Father, without limit
      and to all eternity.

O Saviour of the world, who by thy cross and precious blood hast redeemed us: Save us and help us, we humbly beseech thee, O Lord. *Amen.*

18. Risen Lord

Jesus Christ our Lord,
   designated Son of God in power
   according to the Spirit of holiness
   by his resurrection from the dead.
                        Romans 1 : 4

Blessed be the God and Father of our Lord Jesus Christ!
   By his great mercy we have been born anew
          to a living hope
   through the resurrection of Jesus Christ
          from the dead,
   and to an inheritance which is imperishable,
       undefiled, and unfading,
       kept in heaven for you,
   who by God's power are guarded through faith
   for a salvation ready to be revealed
             in the last time.
                1 Peter 1 : 3–5

But in fact Christ has been raised from the dead,
   the first fruits of those who have fallen asleep.
For as by a man came death, by a man has come also
   the resurrection of the dead.
For as in Adam all die, so also in Christ
   shall all be made alive.
               1 Corinthians 15 : 20–22

Lo, I am with you always, to the close of the age.
                    Matthew 28 : 20

Easter Praise

73.   THOU ART RISEN, O LORD!
       Let the gospel trumpets speak,
          and the news as of holy fire,
          burning and flaming and inextinguishable,
          run to the ends of the earth.

THOU ART RISEN, O LORD!
  Let all creation greet the good tidings
    with jubilant shout;
    for its redemption has come,
    the long night is past, the Saviour lives!
    and rides and reigns in triumph
      now and unto the ages of ages.

74. THANKS BE UNTO THEE, O CHRIST,
    because thou hast broken for us
      the bonds of sin
    and brought us into fellowship
      with the Father.
  Thanks be unto thee, O Christ,
    because thou hast overcome death
      and opened to us
      the gates of eternal life.
  Thanks be unto thee, O Christ,
    because where two or three are gathered together
      in thy name
    there art thou in the midst of them.
  Thanks be unto thee, O Christ,
    because thou ever livest
    to make intercession for us.
  For these and all other benefits
    of thy mighty resurrection,
  thanks be unto thee, O Christ.

Easter Prayers
75. O GOD, who by the glorious death and resurrection
      of thy Son Jesus Christ,
    hast brought life and immortality to light:
  Grant us so to die daily unto sin
    that we may evermore live with thee
    in the joy of his resurrection;
    through the same Jesus Christ our Lord,
    to whom be glory and dominion
      for ever and ever.

76.   GRANT UNTO US, O GOD, to trust thee
             not for ourselves alone
          but for those also whom we love
             and who are hid from us
             by the shadow of death;
          that, as we believe thy power to have raised
             our Lord Jesus Christ from the dead,
             so we may trust thy love
             to give eternal life
             to all who believe in him;
          through the same Jesus Christ our Lord.

The eye of faith
   Open the eyes of my spirit, dear Lord, to see you always
      present, so that I may converse with you, and walk with
      you to the eternal home of the Father.

77.   THE GOD OF PEACE,
             that brought again from the dead
                our Lord Jesus,
             that great shepherd of the sheep,
                through the blood of the
                everlasting covenant,
             make us perfect in every good work
                to do his will,
             working in us that which is
             well-pleasing in his sight;
                through Jesus Christ,
             to whom be glory for ever and ever. *Amen.*

19. King of Glory

Enthroned in glory

Worthy is the Lamb who was slain, to receive power and
wealth and wisdom and might and honour and glory
and blessing.

To him who sits upon the throne and to the Lamb be
blessing and honour and glory and might for ever ...

Revelation 5 : 12–13

Yet ever present

He who descended is he who also ascended far above all
heavens, that he might fill all things.

Ephesians 4 : 10

Ever praying for us

Since then we have a great high priest who has passed
through the heavens, Jesus, the Son of God, let us hold
fast our confession.

For we have not a high priest who is unable to sympathize
with our weaknesses, but one who in every respect has
been tempted as we are, yet without sinning.

Let us then with confidence draw near to the throne of
grace, that we may receive mercy and find grace to help
in time of need.

Hebrews 4 : 14–16

Preparing a place for us

Let not your hearts be troubled; believe in God, believe
also in me.

In my Father's house are many rooms; if it were not so,
would I have told you that I go to prepare a place for
you?

And when I go and prepare a place for you, I will come
again and I will take you to myself, that where I am
you may be also.

John 14 : 1–3

Meditation

Our hearts can be full of joy and confidence
because Christ reigns
on the throne of the universe,
adored by angels and saints.
From his throne he orders his kingdom
and pours down on his people
his Holy Spirit.
As he gave his life on the cross
so now he offers
that once-for-all perfect, eternal sacrifice
in heaven,
for ever interceding
for us who know and love him,
and for all who have not yet
availed themselves of God's saving love.

Acts of Worship

78.   Lift our hearts and minds to thy presence, O God,
where our Saviour Christ is ever with thee
in the centre of power,
the centre of love,
the centre of saving activity,
and where it is thy will
that our human nature too shall be
sanctified and fulfilled,
gathered into the divine love
and blessed to all eternity.

79.   Therefore with angels and archangels,
and with all the company of heaven,
we laud and magnify thy glorious name;
evermore praising thee, and saying,
Holy, Holy, Holy,
Lord God of hosts,
heaven and earth are full of thy glory.
Glory be to thee, O Lord most high.

80. O Lord, the King of Glory,
      who through the eternal doors didst ascend
         to thy Father's throne,
      and open the kingdom of heaven to all believers;
    grant that, whilst thou dost reign in heaven,
    we may not be bowed down to the things of earth,
      but that our hearts may be lifted up
      whither thou, our redemption, art gone before;
    who with the Father and the Holy Spirit,
         livest and reignest,
  ever one God, world without end.

81. O Glorious Christ, who in thy ascension didst enter
         into thy kingdom;
    Remember, we pray thee, the countless millions
      who have not heard of the redemption
        which thou hast won for them.
    Grant that they may learn, through thy church,
        of the new and living way
        which thou hast opened for them.
    Let them draw near in fullness of faith,
      to enter with thee into the holy place
        of the Father's presence,
      and receive forgiveness and peace.
    So may they worship,
      with the innumerable company of angels
      and with the spirits of just men made perfect,
    Father, Son and Holy Spirit, one God,
        blessed for evermore.

My heart rejoices
  with you, O Lord Christ, in the Father's acceptance of
    your life and death, your sacrifice of love, your presence
    with him, and your unceasing love for us.

82. Unto him that sitteth on the throne,
        and unto the Lamb,
      be the blessing and the honour,
      and the glory, and the dominion,
        for ever and ever. *Amen.*

20. New Life in Christ

Truly, truly, I say to you, unless one is born of water and the
  Spirit, he cannot enter the kingdom of God.
That which is born of the flesh is flesh, and that which is
  born of the Spirit is spirit.

John 3 : 5–6

And Peter said to them,
  Repent, and be baptized every one of you in the name of
Jesus Christ for the forgiveness of your sins; and you shall
receive the gift of the Holy Spirit. For the promise is to
you and to your children and to all that are far off, every
one whom the Lord our God calls to him.

Acts 2 : 38–39

I am the vine, you are the branches.
He who abides in me, and I in him, he it is that bears much
  fruit, for apart from me you can do nothing.
Abide in me, and I in you. As the branch cannot bear fruit
  by itself, unless it abides in the vine, neither can you,
  unless you abide in me.

John 15 : 5, 4

Do you know that all of us who have been baptized into
  Christ Jesus were baptized into his death?
We were buried therefore with him by baptism into death, so
  that as Christ was raised from the dead by the glory of the
  Father, we too might walk in newness of life.

Romans 6 : 3–4

Let us pray
  for all who are preparing for baptism,
      that they may give themselves wholly to Christ,
      that they may let Christ transform their lives;
  for all who help to prepare new converts for baptism;

for all baptized in infancy,
　　that parents, godparents and the Christian community
　　in each place may help them to grow up in Christ, in
　　steadfast fear and love;
for all whom Christ is calling,
　　that they may have the courage to confess him before
　　men.

Let me keep close
　　to you, O Christ, knowing that you have taken me into
　　your divine being, into the deathless love of the
　　Godhead.

Let us remember
　　the day when we ourselves were baptized
　　　　and became members of Christ,
　　　　　　children of God,
　　　　and inheritors of the kingdom of heaven.

83.　ALMIGHTY AND EVERLASTING GOD,
　　　　we thank thee that thou hast received us
　　　　into the fold of thy church.
　　　　　　Let thy Spirit be upon us
　　　　　　and dwell in us for ever.
　　　　　　Keep us, we entreat thee,
　　　　　　under thy fatherly care and protection;
　　　　　　　　guide us and sanctify us
　　　　　　　　both in body and soul.
　　　Enrich us abundantly with thy heavenly grace,
　　　and lead us to witness a good confession,
　　　and to persevere therein to the end,
　　　　　　through Jesus Christ our Lord.

84.　WE HUMBLY BESEECH THEE, O LORD,
　　　　that we who have been made thy children
　　　　　　by adoption and grace,
　　　　　　being dead unto sin
　　　　　　may live unto righteousness,

58

and being buried with Christ in his death
   may crucify the old man,
and utterly abolish the whole body of sin;
and that, as we are made partakers of the death
      of thy Son,
so we may also be partakers of his resurrection:
   through the same Jesus Christ our Lord.

85.   ALMIGHTY AND EVERLASTING GOD,
   whose beloved Son became man
     for us men and for our salvation,
   and gave commandment to his disciples
   that they should go and teach all nations,
   and baptize them in the name of the Father
   and of the Son and of the Holy Spirit:
Give us grace to be obedient to his command,
and grant that all men may have new birth in him,
and, being delivered out of the power of darkness,
   may be received into the kingdom of thy love:
   through the same Jesus Christ our Lord.

86.   THE LORD JESUS CHRIST be near thee to defend thee,
within thee to refresh thee, around thee to preserve
thee, before thee to guide thee, behind thee to justify
thee, above thee to bless thee; who liveth and reigneth with the Father and the Holy Spirit, God for
evermore. *Amen.*

21. Christ our Food

Jesus said to them,
>I am the bread of life; he who comes to me shall not hunger, and he who believes in me shall never thirst . . .
>I am the living bread which came down from heaven; if any one eats of this bread, he will live for ever; and the bread which I shall give for the life of the world is my flesh . . . Truly, truly, I say to you,
>unless you eat the flesh of the Son of man and drink his blood you have no life in you . . . He who eats my flesh and drinks my blood abides in me, and I in him.

John 6 : 35, 51, 53, 56

I am unwilling to send them away hungry, lest they faint on the way.
Matthew 15 : 32

Arise and eat, else the journey will be too great for you.
1 Kings 19 : 7

For I [Paul] received from the Lord what I also delivered to you, that the Lord Jesus on the night when he was betrayed took bread, and when he had given thanks, he broke it, and said,
>This is my body which is for you. Do this in remembrance of me.

In the same way also the cup, after supper, saying,
>This cup is the new covenant in my blood. Do this, as often as you drink it, in remembrance of me.

For as often as you eat this bread and drink the cup, you proclaim the Lord's death until he comes.
1 Corinthians 11 : 23–26

Behold, I stand at the door and knock; if any one hears my voice and opens the door, I will come in to him and eat with him, and he with me.
Revelation 3 : 20

Let us reflect how in the Holy Communion
        the night of Christ's birth,
        the night in which he was betrayed,
        the hours upon the cross,
        the morning of resurrection,
        the glory of the ascension,
        and our own worship and need
    are brought together in one eternal moment.

Let us thank God that throughout the world
        the Holy Communion is the most loved and
        solemn act of Christian worship;
    that in this sacrament Christ comes to us in forgiveness
        and love, to unite us to himself, to transform us for
        his service.
Let us offer an act of deepest penitence that Christians of
    different churches are not yet able to meet together in
    unity at the Lord's table.

We come at Christ's command
87.   LORD, THIS IS THY FEAST,
        prepared by thy longing,
        spread at thy command,
        attended at thine invitation,
        blessed by thine own word,
        distributed by thine own hand,
        the undying memorial of thy sacrifice
            upon the cross,
        the full gift of thine everlasting love,
        and its perpetuation till time shall end.

    LORD, this is bread of heaven, bread of life,
        that, whoso eateth, never shall hunger more.
        And this the cup of pardon, healing, gladness,
            strength,
        that, whoso drinketh, thirsteth not again.
    So may we come, O Lord, to thy table;
        Lord Jesu, come to us.

88. IT IS VERILY meet and right, holy and becoming,
        Lord God, Father Almighty,
     to worship thee, to hymn thee, to give thanks unto thee,
        to return thee praise both night and day,
     with unceasing mouths, and lips that keep not silence,
        and hearts that cannot be still.

We ask for sanctifying grace
89. STRENGTHEN, O LORD, the hands which have been
        stretched out to receive thy holy things, that they
        may daily bring forth fruit to thy divine glory.
     Grant that the ears which have heard thy songs may be
        closed to the voice of clamour and dispute;
           that the eyes which have seen thy great love may also
              uphold thy blessed hope;
           that the tongues which have uttered thy praise may
              speak the truth;
           that the feet which have walked in thy courts may
              walk in the region of light;
           that the souls and bodies which have fed upon thy
              living body may be restored to newness of life.
     And with us may thy great love for ever abide,
        that we may abundantly render back praise,
        praise to thy sovereignty.

90. AND HERE WE OFFER AND PRESENT UNTO THEE ourselves,
        our souls and bodies, to be a reasonable, holy, and
        living sacrifice; and we pray thee to fulfil in us, and
        in all people, the purpose of thy redeeming love;
        through Jesus Christ our Lord. *Amen.*

Grace after food
     O bread of heaven and wine of the soul, I thank you for
     your unfailing nourishing of my inner being.

IV. MAKING MEN WHOLE

22. Lord, What is Man?

What is man, that thou art mindful of him, and the son of man that thou visitest him?

Bible answers—
91.
A creature made by God
The image of God
A servant of God
A child of God
A sinner in need of forgiveness
The brother for whom Christ died
A member of Christ's body
A friend of God
A fellow worker with God
A temple of the Holy Spirit
A partaker of the divine nature
An heir of eternal life.

Human experience answers—
92. AN EMBODIED BEING
a thinking being
a feeling being
a spiritual being
a social being
a responsible being
a being on the way.

What shall I render unto the Lord for all his benefits toward me?
93.
My reverence as a creature
My receptiveness to the divine impress
My duty as a servant

My love as a son
My penitence as a sinner
My gratitude as a brother redeemed
My joy in my fellow members
My understanding as a friend
My co-operation as a fellow worker
My welcome as his dwelling-place
My desire to be like him
My thankfulness as an heir
My life now and for ever.

94. PRAISE THE LORD, O MY SOUL,
    and all that is within me praise his holy name.
Praise the Lord, O my soul,
    and forget not all his benefits;
        who forgiveth all thy sin
        and healeth all thine infirmities;
who saveth thy life from destruction
and crowneth thee with mercy and lovingkindness.

95. BLESSED BE THE LORD GOD of Israel
    for he hath visited and redeemed his people . . .
    to give knowledge of salvation unto his people
        for the remission of their sins,
        through the tender mercy of our God
        whereby the day-spring from on high
            hath visited us,
        to give light to them that sit in darkness,
            and in the shadow of death,
        and to guide our feet into the way of peace.

Let the divine seed
    of your own being, planted in me at my birth, O Creator
    Lord, germinate and grow until I become what you
    intend me to be.

64

96. ALMIGHTY GOD, who didst wonderfully create man in thine own image, and didst yet more wonderfully restore him: Grant, we beseech thee, that as thy Son, our Lord Jesus Christ was made in the likeness of men, so we may be made partakers of the divine nature; through the same thy Son, who with thee and the Holy Spirit liveth and reigneth, one God, world without end. *Amen.*

23. Wilt thou be made whole?

I came that they may have life, and have it abundantly.

John 10 : 10

As he passed by, he saw a man blind from his birth.

And his disciples asked him, Rabbi, who sinned, this man or his parents, that he was born blind?

Jesus answered, It was not that this man sinned, or his parents, but that the works of God might be made manifest in him.

John 9 : 1–3

And preach as you go, saying, The kingdom of heaven is at hand. Heal the sick, raise the dead, cleanse lepers, cast out demons. You received without pay, give without pay.

Matthew 10 : 7–8

Let us thank God
> that all down the ages the church has followed her Master's example in caring for the sick and suffering;
> for the countless people who have found the God of love through the skill of a missionary doctor or nurse;
> for the selfless service of doctors, nurses, hospital workers, of many races, who show forth God's love in action;
> that through the revealing of the causes of disease and the secrets of health, disease is being mastered and men are finding the abundant life which God wills for them;
> that governments are now accepting responsibility for health and healing.

Let us pray
> for all who suffer, that they may look up in faith to God to receive that strength which shall make them more than conquerors;
> that through the healing work of the church men may be made whole in body, mind and spirit;
> for all medical colleges, hospitals and dispensaries and for all who work and train in them;
> that the church in every land may teach men how to use suffering.

97. GRANT, O LORD, to all those who are bearing pain thy
spirit of healing,
thy spirit of peace and hope,
of courage and endurance.
Cast out from them the spirit of anxiety and fear;
grant them perfect confidence and trust in thee,
that in thy light they may see light;
through Jesus Christ our Lord.

98. MAY THE FATHER BLESS thee,
who created all things in the beginning;
may the SON of God heal thee;
may the HOLY SPIRIT enlighten thee,
guard thy body, save thy soul,
direct thy thoughts,
and bring thee safe to the heavenly country:
who liveth and reigneth
one God, world without end.

For doctors, nurses and health workers
99. O MERCIFUL FATHER, who hast made man's body to be
a temple of thy Holy Spirit: Sanctify, we pray thee,
all those whom thou hast called to study and practise the art of healing and the prevention of disease;
strengthen them in body and soul, and bless their
work, that they may themselves live as members
and servants of Christ, and give comfort to those
whom he lived and died to save; through the same
Jesus Christ our Lord.

Yes, Lord
I want to be made whole, spirit, mind and body integrated, available for you in this life and ready in you for
the life beyond.

100. BLESSED BE GOD, even the Father of our Lord Jesus Christ, the Father of mercies, and the God of all comfort; who comforteth us in all our tribulation, that we may be able to comfort them which are in any trouble, by the comfort wherewith we ourselves are comforted by God. *Amen.*

24. With all your Mind

Hear, O Israel: The Lord our God, the Lord is one;
   and you shall love the Lord your God with all your heart,
   and with all your soul, and with all your mind, and with
   all your strength.

Mark 12 : 29–30

Do not be conformed to this world but be transformed by the
   renewal of your mind, that you may prove what is the will
   of God, what is good and acceptable and perfect.

Romans 12 : 2

Finally, brethren, whatever is true, whatever is honourable,
   whatever is just, whatever is pure, whatever is lovely,
   whatever is gracious, if there is any excellence, if there is
   anything worthy of praise, think about these things.

Philippians 4 : 8

101.   O GOD, who art the goal of all knowledge and the
       source of all truth, who dost lead mankind towards
       thyself along the paths of discovery and learning,
       direct with thy wise spirit the work of education in
       every land. Especially we would pray for those who
       have the difficult task of adapting new knowledge to
       the mind of ancient peoples. Give them insight into
       the needs of those whom they teach, humility to
       learn from their traditions, and wisdom to combine
       the old and the new. Above all, give them that
       grace and beauty of life without which all know-
       ledge is vain.

Let us pray
   that all Christian colleges and schools may be centres of
   Christian worship, learning and community;

for a keen sense of vocation among all teachers;

for the staff and students of training colleges in all lands;

for closer co-operation between church and home and
school in the work of education;

for the guidance of the Holy Spirit in countries where the
church has no direct share in education;

for Christian teachers who work in state schools.

102. O THOU WHO ART THE GOD OF TRUTH AND LIGHT as
well as of love and righteousness: We pray for the
schools and colleges of all countries, that they may
be such homes of fellowship and brotherhood,
learning and culture, that from them shall come
forth a stream of leaders to share these blessings
with their fellow countrymen and to guide their
countries into the way of peace; through Jesus
Christ our Lord.

103. GRANT, O LORD, to all teachers and students,
to love that which is worth loving,
to know that which is worth knowing,
to praise that which pleaseth thee most,
to esteem that which is most precious unto thee,
and to dislike whatsoever is evil in thine eyes.
Grant us with true judgement to distinguish
things that differ,
and above all, to search out and to do
what is well-pleasing unto thee;
through Jesus Christ our Lord.

Let my mind
be trained by your Spirit, O God, so that I may have the
mind of your pattern Son, and look at everyone, everything and every happening through his eyes.

MAY THE PEACE OF GOD dwell in our hearts, and the word of
Christ abide in us richly in all wisdom. *Amen.*

25. You give them something to eat

And when it grew late, his disciples came to him and said,
This is a lonely place, and the hour is now late; send them
away, to go into the country and villages round about and
buy themselves something to eat.
But he answered them,
You give them something to eat.

Mark 6 : 35–37

What does it profit, my brethren, if a man says he has faith
but has not works? Can his faith save him?
If a brother of sister is ill-clad and in lack of daily food, and
one of you says to them, Go in peace, be warmed and
filled, without giving them the things needed for the body,
what does it profit?
So faith by itself, if it has no works, is dead.

James 2 : 14–17

Come, O blessed of my Father, inherit the kingdom prepared
for you from the foundation of the world;
for I was hungry and you gave me food, I was thirsty and
you gave me drink, I was a stranger and you welcomed
me, I was naked and you clothed me, I was sick and you
visited me, I was in prison and you came to me.
Lord, when did we see thee hungry and feed thee, or thirsty
and give thee drink?
As you did it to one of the least of these my brethren, you did
it to me.

Matthew 25 : 34–37, 40

They shall hunger no more, neither thirst any more; the sun
shall not strike them, nor any scorching heat.
For the Lamb in the midst of the throne will be their shepherd, and he will guide them to springs of living water;
and God will wipe away every tear from their eyes.

Revelation 7 : 16, 17

71

Let us remember

that three-fifths of the people of the world do not yet get
enough to eat;

that it is God's will that men should have all things need-
ful for a full and happy life.

Let us thank God

for his wonderful order of creation, for the germ of life in
the seed and for the bounty of harvest;

for the Food and Agriculture Organization of the United
Nations which is working with national governments to
increase food production;

for the growing number of agricultural missionaries who
teach men of many races that the earth belongs to God
and help them to use it rightly.

Let us pray

that nations may become true neighbours

that the church may show men the example of caring for
one another

that the Christian community in every country may work
for social justice and mutual responsibility.

Over to us

You have given us the earth, the fertility of the soil, rain
and sunshine, the life in the seed and its power of
growth. Enough for all, dear Lord, if we renounce
greed.

104.   ALMIGHTY AND EVERLASTING GOD, who hast graciously
given to us the fruits of the earth in their season, we
yield thee humble and hearty thanks for these thy
bounties, beseeching thee to give us grace rightly to
use them to thy glory and the relief of those that
need; through Jesus Christ our Lord.

105.   GIVE, O LORD, to all who till the ground
           wisdom to understand thy laws,
           and to co-operate with thy wise ordering
               of the world;
       and grant that the bountiful fruits of the earth
           may not be hoarded by the selfish
           or squandered by the foolish,
       but that all who work may share abundantly
           in the harvest of the soil;
           through Jesus Christ our Lord.

106.   ALMIGHTY GOD, who fillest the earth with thy riches
           for the use of all thy children,
       have regard, we pray thee, to the impoverishment
               of the nations;
           and on all who are in authority
           bestow thy gifts of wisdom and goodwill,
           that, being lifted above self-regard,
           they may establish a new order,
       wherein the needs of all men shall be supplied;
           through Jesus Christ our Lord.

107.   BLESSED BE THOU, O GOD,
           who bringest food out of the earth
           and makest the hearts of men glad
               with thy goodness.
       Blessed be thou, for ever and ever. *Amen.*

26. Peace on Earth

Peace is God's gift to his people

Let me hear what God the Lord will speak, for he will speak peace to his people, to his saints, to those who turn to him in their hearts.

Surely his salvation is at hand for those who fear him, that glory may dwell in our land.

Steadfast love and faithfulness will meet; righteousness and peace will kiss each other.

Psalm 85 : 8–10

Peace is promised to all in Christ

For to us a child is born, to us a son is given;

and the government will be upon his shoulder, and his name will be called Wonderful Counsellor, Mighty God, Everlasting Father, Prince of Peace.

Of the increase of his government and of peace there will be no end, upon the throne of David, and over his kingdom, to establish it, and to uphold it with justice and with righteousness from this time forth and for evermore.

The zeal of the Lord of hosts will do this.

Isaiah 9 : 6–7

Men fail to recognize where true peace lies

And when he drew near and saw the city he wept over it, saying,

Would that even today you knew the things that make for peace! But now they are hid from your eyes.

For the days shall come upon you when your enemies will cast up a bank about you and surround you, and hem you in on every side, and dash you to the ground, you and your children within you, and they will not leave one stone upon another in you; because you did not know the time of your visitation.

Luke 19 : 41–44

Let us pray

    that governments and peoples may continue to confer together and to look for ways of removing fear and suspicion;

    for a determined effort to secure a higher standard of living in poorer and developing countries;

    that statesmen and leaders of public opinion may refrain from words and actions which stir up enmity and hatred;

    that representatives of the churches in countries between which tension exists may promote reconciliation;

    that Christians everywhere may unite in Christ's ministry of reconciliation;

    for insight to recognize the seeds of strife in our own national prejudices and our self-righteousness;

    that the nations of the world may understand and seek the things that belong to peace—truth, justice, freedom, patience and goodwill.

For the leaders of the nations

108. ALMIGHTY GOD,

    from whom all thoughts of truth and peace proceed:
      Kindle, we pray thee, in the hearts of all men
        the true love of peace,
      and guide with thy pure and peaceable wisdom
      those who take counsel for the nations of the earth;
    that in tranquillity thy kingdom may go forward,
    till the earth is filled with the knowledge of thy love;
      through Jesus Christ our Lord.

For an end to war

109. MAY THE MEMORY of two world wars strengthen our efforts for peace;

    May the memory of those who died inspire
    our service to the living;

May the memory of past destruction move us
　　to build for the future;
O Father of souls,
O God of peace,
O builder of the kingdom.

Finally, let us pray for ourselves
110.　LORD, make us instruments of thy peace.
　　　Where there is hatred, let us sow love;
　　　where there is injury, pardon;
　　　where there is discord, union;
　　　where there is doubt, faith;
　　　where there is despair, hope;
　　　where there is darkness, light;
　　　where there is sadness, joy;
　　for thy mercy and for thy truth's sake.

Lord, we know
　　that if there is no peace in the hearts of men, there will be
　　　no peace on earth. Let your peace be in my heart, and
　　　go out to others in ever widening circles of love.

111.　NOW THE GOD OF PEACE,
　　　that brought again from the dead our Lord Jesus,
　　　　that great shepherd of the sheep,
　　　through the blood of the everlasting covenant,
　　make us perfect in every good work to do his will,
　　　　working in us
　　　that which is well-pleasing in his sight,
　　　　through Jesus Christ;
　　　to whom be glory for ever and ever. *Amen.*

27. The New Humanity

The unity of mankind in Christ foretold
  I saw in the night visions,
    and behold, with the clouds of heaven
        there came one like a son of man,
      and he came to the Ancient of Days
          and was presented before him.
And to him was given dominion and glory and kingdom,
that all peoples, nations, and languages should serve him;
    his dominion is an everlasting dominion,
        which shall not pass away,
and his kingdom one that shall not be destroyed.

Daniel 7 : 13, 14

The enmity between men abolished in Christ
          But now in Christ Jesus
    you (Gentiles) who once were far off have been brought
          near in the blood of Christ.
          For he is our peace,
        who has made us both (Jew and Gentile) one,
    and has broken down the dividing wall of hostility,
      by abolishing in his flesh
      the law of commandments and ordinances,
    that he might create in himself one new man
          in place of the two,
          so making peace,
      and might reconcile us both to God
      in one body through the cross,
      thereby bringing the hostility to an end.
And he came and preached peace to you who were far off
          and peace to those who were near;
      for through him we both have access
          in one Spirit to the Father.

Ephesians 2 : 13–18

77

In Christ we are all born again,
so all distinctions are done away
>You have put on the new nature,
>>which is being renewed in knowledge
>>after the image of its creator.
>Here there cannot be Greek and Jew,
>>circumcised and uncircumcised,
>>barbarian, Scythian, slave, free man,
>>but Christ is all, and in all.
>Put on then, as God's chosen ones,
>>holy and beloved,
>>compassion, kindness, lowliness,
>>meekness, and patience.

Colossians 3 : 10–12

Let us pray
>that the mind of Christ
>>may be in us
>to overcome all prejudice and self-consciousness
>>of race or colour or tongue;
>for grace to bear no resentment
>>when we or our fellow countrymen
>>are criticized;
>>for humility to examine ourselves
>>to see if there is any truth
>>in what is brought against us;
>for a readiness to open hearth and home
>>to people of other races,
>especially to strangers visiting our country;
>for our brethren in countries where racial tension is acute,
>>that they may work
>>with patience and understanding to abolish
>all forms of segregation and discrimination.

Let us thank God
>for the new race of men which is created in Jesus Christ, in
>which the power of the Holy Spirit overcomes
>>racial pride and fear;

78

that within every nation there are
Christians whose supreme loyalty is to
> Christ as Lord
and who recognize all men as brothers in him.

You break down
> all dividing walls of hostility, O Christ, and rend all cur-
> tains of prejudice. Let me be like you, a universal
> brother to all.

Let us pray for racial reconciliation
112. FATHER, who hast made all men in thy likeness
> and lovest all whom thou hast made,
>> suffer not our family to separate itself from thee
>> by building barriers of race and colour.
> As thy Son our Saviour was born of a
>> Hebrew mother,
>>> but rejoiced in the faith of a Syrian woman
>>> and of a Roman soldier,
>>>> welcomed the Greeks who sought him,
>>>> and suffered a man from Africa
>>>>> to carry his cross,
>>> so teach us to regard the members of all races
>>> as fellow heirs of the kingdom
>>> of Jesus Christ our Lord.

113. WE PRAY THEE, O GOD,
>> to breathe into the students of this day
>> such brave magnanimity of thought and speech
>>> that righteousness in every land may speak
>>> with the clear voice of truth,
>>> and that the universities of all countries
>>> may not fail to raise up leaders
>>> bold and able to bring the nations
>>> into the ways of justice, brotherhood
>>>> and peace.
>> We ask it in his name
>>> who came to give life more abundantly,
>>>> Jesus Christ our Lord.

114. GOD OF ALL NATIONS,
  we pray thee for all the people of thy earth;
   for those who are consumed in mutual hatred
    and bitterness;
   for those who make war upon their neighbours;
   for those who tyrannously oppress;
   for those who groan under cruelty and subjection.
  We beseech thee to teach mankind to live together
   in peace;
   no man exploiting the weak,
   no man hating the strong,
   each race working out its own destiny,
    unfettered, self-respecting, fearless.
  Teach us to be worthy of freedom,
   free from social wrong,
   free from individual oppression
    and contempt,
   pure of heart and hand,
   despising none, defrauding none,
  giving to all men—in all dealings of life—
  the honour we owe to those who are thy children,
  whatever their colour, their race, or their caste.

  AND NOW MAY THE BLESSING OF THE LORD
  rest and remain upon all his people
   in every land, of every tongue. *Amen.*

28. Leavening Society

The kingdom of heaven is like leaven which a woman took
and hid in three measures of meal, till it was all leavened.

Matthew 13 : 33

Do you not know that a little leaven ferments the whole
lump of dough? Cleanse out the old leaven that you may
be fresh dough, as you really are unleavened.
For Christ, our paschal lamb, has been sacrificed.
Let us, therefore, celebrate the festival, not with the old
leaven, the leaven of malice and evil, but with the
unleavened bread of sincerity and truth.

1 Corinthians 5 : 6–8

You are the salt of the earth; but if salt has lost its taste, how
shall its saltness be restored? It is no longer good for anything except to be thrown out and trodden under foot by
men.
You are the light of the world. A city set on a hill cannot be
hid. Nor do men light a lamp and put it under a bushel,
but on a stand, and it gives light to all in the house.
Let your light shine before men, that they may see your good
works and give glory to your Father who is in heaven.

Matthew 5 : 13–16

Let us pray
that in every nation Christians may be as salt, cleansing
the national life, preserving all that is good, giving tone
and character;
that Christians may give such selfless service to their own
country that others may be brought to the faith which
inspires such insight and service.

O God
> let me be worth your salt, as well as my own.

115. WE PRAY THEE, O LORD, that thou wilt so reveal
thyself in us, that through us men may be drawn to
the love of thee. May the world not mould us today,
but may we be strengthened to help mould the
world; through Jesus Christ our Lord.

116. O GOD, who hast bound us together in this bundle of
life, give us grace to understand how our lives
depend upon the courage, the industry, the honesty,
the integrity of our fellow men; that we may be
mindful of their needs, grateful for their faithfulness,
and faithful in our responsibilities to them; through
Jesus Christ our Lord.

117. LORD JESUS CHRIST
alive and at large in the world
help me to follow and find you there today
in the places where I work
meet people
spend money
and make plans.
Take me as a disciple of your kingdom
to see through your eyes
and hear the questions you are asking
to welcome all with your trust and truth,
and to change the things that contradict God's love
by the power of your cross
and the freedom of your Spirit.

118. Now UNTO HIM that is able to do exceeding
abundantly above all that we ask or think,
according to the power that worketh in us,
unto him be glory in the church by Christ Jesus,
throughout all ages, world without end. *Amen.*

V. ONE FAITH, ONE CHURCH, ONE WORLD

29. The Bible

Whatever was written in former days was written for our instruction, that by steadfastness and by the encouragement of the scriptures we might have hope.

Romans 15 : 4

O foolish men, and slow of heart to believe all that the prophets have spoken! Was it not necessary that the Christ should suffer these things and enter into his glory?
And beginning with Moses and all the prophets, he interpreted to them in all the scriptures the things concerning himself.

Luke 24 : 25–27

You have heard that it was said to the men of old . . . but I say to you . . .

Matthew 5 : 22–24 (repeated three times)

But we have this treasure in earthen vessels, to show that the transcendent power belongs to God.

2 Corinthians 4 : 7

For the written code kills, but the Spirit gives life.

2 Corinthians 3 : 6

Let us thank God

for the good news that has come to us through the scriptures, and for the light and strength that come from our
study of them

that the Bible is the most loved, the best studied, and the
most widely distributed of all books

that believers in God in earlier generations believed that
they heard God speaking to them in their own hearts,
interpreted his word to them relevantly to their own
times, obeyed the word so received, and bequeathed
their witness for later generations of faith,

that the Holy Spirit is always bringing out deeper meaning and new relevance, correcting what may be mis-
taken or temporary, and enlarging earlier ideas of God.

that in Jesus we receive God's revelation and incarnation
in a personal life by which we can judge all thinking
about God.

119. O GOD, creator of the heart in man, we thank thee
that thou dost speak to us thy creatures in the language of the heart, so that everyone hears thee in his
own thought-forms and language. In thee the Babel of
languages becomes simplified in the language of
Pentecost, and all men may hear of thy wonderful
deeds and thy saving love, longed for by prophets in
the past and now made clear in thy blessed Son Jesus
Christ, our Lord.

Let us pray

120. BLESSED LORD,
who hast caused all holy scriptures
to be written for our learning:
Grant that we may in such wise hear them,
read, mark, learn, and inwardly digest them,
that by patience,
and comfort of thy holy word,

we may embrace and ever hold fast
the blessed hope of eternal life,
which thou hast given us
in our Saviour Jesus Christ.

121. ALMIGHTY AND MOST MERCIFUL GOD,
who hast given the Bible to be the revelation
of thy great love to man,
and of thy power and will to save him:
Grant that our study of it may not be made in vain
by the callousness or carelessness of our hearts,
but that by it we may be confirmed in penitence,
lifted to hope,
made strong for service,
and, above all, filled with the true knowledge of thee
and of thy Son Jesus Christ.

122. SPIRIT OF TRUTH, grant that in our dependence on the
scriptures we may never make them a substitute for thee,
but be led to understand thy dealings with earlier
seekers for truth, and so be led into deeper truth,
wider relevance, keener awareness of thy now-
developing purpose. We ask this through him in
whom thy Word and love became incarnate, even
Jesus Christ, our teacher and our Lord.

Let us pray
that we may never be so ossified in the experience and
formulation of earlier generations that we fail to receive
the further inspiration of the Spirit
that we may approach with interest and reverence the
scriptures of other faiths, and see their relevance to our
own, that thy Spirit may bless and guide Bible scholars,
translators and publishers, so that all may receive the
heritage of the past and inspiration for the future.

O Holy Spirit, let me see the spirit and not the letter only: let me perceive your developing truth and hear your voice speaking to me today.

123. THE GOD OF HOPE fill us with all joy and peace in believing, that we may abound in hope, in the power of the Holy Spirit.

30. The Body of Christ

Our Lord speaks of the relationship
between himself and his disciples

I am the true vine, and my Father is the vinedresser.

Every branch of mine that bears no fruit, he takes away, and every branch that does bear fruit he prunes, that it may bear more fruit.

You are already made clean by the word which I have spoken to you.

Abide in me, and I in you. As the branch cannot bear fruit by itself, unless it abides in the vine, neither can you, unless you abide in me.

I am the vine, you are the branches.

He who abides in me, and I in him, he it is that bears much fruit, for apart from me you can do nothing.

John 15 : 1–5

Paul speaks of the church as the body of Christ

For just as the body is one and has many members, and all the members of the body, though many, are one body, so it is with Christ.

For by one Spirit we were all baptized into one body— Jews or Greeks, slaves or free—and all were made to drink of one Spirit . . .

Now you are the body of Christ and individually members of it.

1 Corinthians 12 : 12–14, 27

Each of us has his own work to do in the church,
the body of Christ

And his gifts were that some should be apostles,
> some prophets, some evangelists,
> some pastors and teachers,
for the equipment of the saints,
for the work of ministry,
for building up the body of Christ,

until we all attain to the unity of the faith
and of the knowledge of the Son of God,
to mature manhood,
to the measure of the stature of the fullness of Christ.

Ephesians 4 : 11–13

Meditation

The church is the visible organ through which the
ascended Christ now lives and works among men as he
once did through his human body;

Christ did these things while he was here on earth—
he revealed God;
he healed men;
he brought them forgiveness;
he loved them; he died for thcm;
he rescued them from the power of evil;
he cleansed and strengthened human nature.

Christ is the head whom all the members of the body obey;
disobedience in any of the limbs means paralysis.

Our relationship to one another is one of fellow members
of the body, all working in harmony for the whole body
in obedience to the head.

Let us pray

124. GRANT, O LORD GOD, that thy church,
as it hath one foundation and one head,
may verily and indeed be one body,
holding one faith, proclaiming one truth,
and following one Lord in holiness of living and
love,
even thy Son our Saviour Jesus Christ.

88

125. ALMIGHTY AND EVER-LIVING GOD,
    we most heartily thank thee that we are
    very members incorporate in the mystical body
        of thy Son,
    which is the blessed company of all faithful people.
  And we most humbly beseech thee, O heavenly
        Father,
    so to assist us with thy grace,
    that we may continue in this holy fellowship,
      and do all such good works
      as thou hast prepared for us to walk in;
    through Jesus Christ our Lord.

126. ETERNAL GOD,
    look mercifully upon the broken body
        of thy church.
      Draw its members unto thee
        and one to another
        by the bands of thy love;
    that its restored unity may bring healing
        to the nations,
    and the life of mankind may glorify thee;
      through Jesus Christ our Lord.

O Lord of the church
  Continue your work on it, making it holy so that through
  it you may further your plan of saving love.

127. ETERNAL FATHER,
    of whom the whole family in heaven and earth is
        named:
      Unite us, as we worship thee here,
        with all who in far-off places
        are lifting up their hands and hearts to thee;
    that thy church throughout the world,
        with the church in heaven,
    may offer up one sacrifice of thanksgiving;
    to the praise and honour of thy holy name.

31. As I have loved you

The two great commandments

You shall love the Lord your God with all your heart, and
  with all your soul, and with all your mind, and with all
  your strength. The second is this,
You shall love your neighbour as yourself.
There is no other commandment greater than these.

Mark 12 : 30–31

A new commandment I give to you, that you love one
  another; even as I have loved you, that you also love
  one another.

John 13 : 34

Love is very patient, very kind. Love knows no jealousy;
love makes no parade, gives itself no airs, is never rude,
never selfish, never irritated, never resentful;
  love is never glad when others go wrong,
love is gladdened by goodness, always slow to expose,
  always eager to believe the best, always hopeful, always
  patient.
Love never disappears.

1 Corinthians 13 : 4–8 (Moffatt)

Meditation

Our Lord commands us not only to love our fellow men as
  ourselves, but to love them as he has loved us.
God's love for us is completely self-giving, without any
  thought of our worth to God or of our being worthy of
  love; love even for the loveless and unlovable.
This selfless love is the gift of the Holy Spirit; Paul calls it
  the greatest of all gifts. We should desire it earnestly,
  and unceasingly ask God to give it to us.
It is love which will win men to God more than anything
  else.

128. O LORD, who hast taught us that all our doings without love are worth nothing: Send thy Holy Spirit,
and pour into our hearts that most excellent gift of
love, the very bond of peace and of all virtues, without which whosoever liveth is counted dead before
thee: Grant this for thine only Son Jesus Christ's
sake.

129. LORD, if we love thee
for the pleasure that we receive
then we but love ourselves;
But if we love thee
to do thee pleasure again,
then let us rejoice to obey thee,
and, for thy sake, to love our brethren;
them that are good
to support them in goodness,
them that are ignorant or careless or evil
to draw them to good,
to be unto all our neighbours
as Christ unto us; for his mercy's sake.

130. O LORD, grant us to love thee:
grant that we may love those that love thee;
grant that we may do the deeds that win thy love.
A prayer of Muhammad

Help the church to be
a community of love, O Christ, in which people may see
the divine pattern for the life of the world.

131. O CHRIST OUR GOD, dwell in our hearts,
that we, being rooted and grounded in love,
and understanding with all the saints
what is the breadth and length and depth and height;
and knowing the love of God which passeth
knowledge
may be filled with all thy fullness. *Amen.*

91

32. Even so I send you

Jesus said to them,

> Peace be with you. As the Father has sent me, even so I send you.

And when he had said this, he breathed on them, and said, Receive the Holy Spirit. If you forgive the sins of any, they are forgiven; if you retain the sins of any, they are retained.

John 20 : 21–23

And Jesus came and said to them,

> All authority in heaven and on earth has been given to me. Go therefore and make disciples of all nations, baptizing them in the name of the Father and of the Son and of the Holy Spirit, teaching them to observe all that I have commanded you; and lo, I am with you always, to the close of the age.

Matthew 28 : 18–20

And he said to them,

> Go into all the world and preach the gospel to the whole creation.

Mark 16 : 15

Thus it is written . . . that repentance and forgiveness of sins should be preached in his name to all nations, beginning from Jerusalem.

Luke 24 : 46–47

But you shall receive power when the Holy Spirit has come upon you; and you shall be my witnesses in Jerusalem and in all Judea and Samaria and to the end of the earth.

Acts 1 : 8

Meditation

All four evangelists record our Lord's command to take part in his mission to the world.

It is the Risen Lord, to whom all power and authority are given, who sends his apostles out.

The mission is to start where the disciples are and spread outwards: where each Christian is—his own country— neighbouring countries—every country;

not only every country, but every area of thought and society.

We do not go alone: Lo, I am with you always.

We go as bearers of good news, telling men what God has done, inviting them to claim God's gracious promises.

We seek for signs that God has already been at work before we arrived.

Let us pray

132. O GOD, mighty to save, infinite in compassion towards the nations that know thee not, and the tongues which cannot speak thy name: We humbly thank thee that thou hast made the church of thy dear Son the chariot of the gospel, to tell it out among the nations that thou art king, and to bear thy love unto the world's end: and for all thy servants who counted not their lives dear unto them on this employment, and for all peoples newly praising thee, we praise and bless thee, Father, Son, and Holy Spirit, one Lord and God for ever.

133. BESTOW THY BLESSING, we beseech thee, O Lord, upon thy church and thy ministers everywhere.

May increasing multitudes hear thy word, receive it, and live by it. May its power be seen more and more in the lives of them that believe.

So work thy great work, Almighty God, in this our country, and in this our generation, that the doubter may be convinced, the wavering established, the sinful converted and the gainsayer gained;

and grant that at the last, according to thy blessed
word of prophecy, the Lord may be king over all
the earth, one Lord, and his name one; through
Jesus Christ our Lord.

Thanksgiving for the progress of the Gospel

134.   THOU ART WORTHY, O LORD, to receive power,
              and riches
           and wisdom and strength,
        and honour and glory, and blessing.
     Blessed be thy glorious name that thy word has
              sounded forth
     not only in Jerusalem and Antioch, in Athens and
              in Rome;
     but in every place the faith of Christ is spread abroad.
           All glory be to thee.

     For the light of thy everlasting gospel,
        sent to every nation, and kindred,
           and tongue, and people,
        shining so long amongst ourselves;
     for thy church, the pillar and ground of the truth,
        against which the gates of hell have not prevailed;
     for thy gracious word of promise,
     that they that be wise shall shine
        as the brightness of the firmament,
     and they that turn many to righteousness
        as the stars for ever and ever.
           All glory be to thee.

You send us, O Lord
     to love and serve the world and to bring your spirit into
        every relationship of human life.

135.   GOD BE MERCIFUL unto us and bless us;
           and give us grace to know his will,
              and strength to do it,
                 for Jesus Christ's sake. *Amen.*

94

33. That they may be one

Our Lord's own prayer
>Holy Father, keep them in thy name which thou hast given me, that they may be one, even as we are one . . . that they may all be one; even as thou, Father, art in me, and I in thee, that they also may be in us, so that the world may believe that thou hast sent me.

John 17 : 11, 21

>There is one body and one Spirit, just as you were called to the one hope that belongs to your call, one Lord, one faith, one baptism, one God and Father of us all, who is above all and through all and in all.

Ephesians 4 : 4–6

>A new commandment I give to you, that you love one another; even as I have loved you, that you also love one another.
>By this all men will know that you are my disciples, if you have love for one another.

John 13 : 34–35

136.   O Lord Jesus Christ, who didst say to thine apostles,
By this shall all men know that ye are my disciples, if
ye have love one to another:
Heal our divisions, and make us one,
one soul and body in thee;
that men may know us for thy true children,
and believe in thee through us.

Let us confess
> our lack of charity and brotherliness to Christians of other denominations
>
> our past indifference to the need for unity
>
> our denominational pride and prejudice
>
> our responsibility through disunity for delaying the salvation of the world.

Let us pray
> that our search for unity may be based on truth as well as on goodwill and love
>
> for the Holy Spirit's guidance of all efforts for church union
>
> for all churches, that each abandoning error and prejudice may bring its gifts to the one holy, catholic and apostolic church
>
> that each church may be ready to die to itself so that the great new church of God's will may come into being.

Let us thank God
> for the stirring of conscience about our lack of unity
>
> for the growing realization of our common faith
>
> for the growing volume of prayer that God will show the divided parts of the church the way back to unity
>
> for the new churches who have spoken with such conviction of the need for unity
>
> for the ecumenical movement, through which Christians of many denominations are striving to find that unity which Christ wills for his church.

137.　O GOD, who by thy Son Jesus Christ
> dost call the children of thy church
>> into a great and holy unity,
>> even as he is one with thee:
> Turn us again, we beseech thee,
> that we may redeem the years of division,
> and recover in thee what we have lost of ourselves;
>> through the same Jesus Christ our Lord.

138.   O LORD JESUS CHRIST, who didst say to thine apostles,
        Peace I leave with you, my peace I give unto you:
            Regard not our sins, but the faith of thy church,
                and grant it that peace and unity
                which is agreeable to thy will;
                    who livest and reignest
                    with the Father and the Holy Spirit,
                    one God, world without end.

Show us the way, O Lord
    to the unity which is your will, that the world may see
    both the strength of your love and the power of your
    grace.

        Now unto him that is able to do exceeding
                        abundantly
                above all that we ask or think,
                    according to the power that worketh in us,
            unto him be glory in the church
                    and in Christ Jesus
            unto all generations for ever and ever. *Amen.*

34. Growing Together

Christ's will for his church

His gifts were that some should be apostles, some prophets, some evangelists, some pastors and teachers, for the equipment of the saints, for the work of ministry, for building up the body of Christ, until we all attain to the unity of the faith and of the knowledge of the Son of God, to mature manhood, to the measure of the stature of the fullness of Christ; . . . we are to grow up in every way into him who is the head, into Christ, from whom the whole body, joined and knit together by every joint with which it is supplied, when each part is working properly, makes bodily growth and upbuilds itself in love.

Ephesians 4 : 11–13, 15–16

Let us thank God

for the growing realization that disunity is a sin,
   it is hindering Christ's salvation,
   it is an obstacle to God's plans,
   it is holding up world peace,
   it is delaying human unity,
   it is wasting the resources of the church,
   it is grieving the heart of God.

Let us thank him

for the movement towards unity in this century
for the growing agreement in matters of faith and ministry
for the part played by Bible Societies, the Evangelical Alliance, the YMCA, the YWCA, the Student Christian Movement, the WCC and many National Councils of Churches
for the Unit of Dialogue of the WCC in its consultations with peoples of other faiths
for the growing co-operation between churches in coming to the aid of people suffering disasters, social injustice, world hunger and disease.

Let us pray

that the churches may covenant with God and with one another to seek the unity of God's will and his way to achieve it

for the guidance of the Holy Spirit for the Churches' Commission of International Affairs in its efforts for peace between nations

that with their differing traditions of worship the churches may learn from one another how to deepen their worship and spiritual life

for faith to see how the Lord of the church is at work in the church in every age to conform it to his will.

139. ETERNAL AND MERCIFUL GOD, who art the God of peace and not of discord: Have mercy upon thy church, divided in thy service; and grant that we, seeking unity in Christ, and in the truth of thy holy word, with one mind and one mouth may glorify thee, the Father of our Lord Jesus Christ. *Amen.*

Let us pray for renewal of the church

140. SPIRIT OF PROMISE, SPIRIT OF UNITY, we thank thee that thou art also the Spirit of renewal. Renew in the whole church, we pray thee, that passionate desire for the coming of thy kingdom which will unite all Christians in one mission to the world. May we all grow up together into him, who is our head, the Saviour of the world, and our only Lord and Master.

It is in our hands, O Lord

but we need your constant pleading,
prompting, sanctifying, energizing grace.

35. To sum up all things in Christ

For God has made known to us in all wisdom and insight the
    mystery of his will,
according to his purpose which he set forth in Christ
    as a plan for the fullness of time,
to unite all things in him, things in heaven and things on
    earth.

Ephesians 1 : 9–10

For the creation waits with eager longing
    for the revealing of the sons of God;
for the creation was subjected to futility,
    not of its own will
but by the will of him who subjected it in hope;
because the creation itself will be set free
    from its bondage to decay
and obtain the glorious liberty
    of the children of God.

Romans 8 : 19–21

Meditation

All things shall find their goal and perfection in Christ.

No man will find his highest good until he has come face
to face with Christ and accepted Christ's claims.

Not only men, but the whole creation shall find its goal in
Christ. But this depends on all men accepting their
freedom as sons of God and living as such.

Let us pray

that all spheres of man's life and work may be brought
under the rule of Christ:
    politics and government, trade and industry,
    management and labour, agriculture and farming,
    science and invention, art and literature,
        personal relationships.

141. Blessed be thou, O God,
who hast declared that it is thine eternal purpose to
gather in one all things in Christ.
Worthy art thou to receive honour and power and
glory,
for the great love wherewith thou hast loved all
mankind,
and hast delivered us from the powers of darkness,
and brought us into the kingdom of thy Son.

142. Yea, O Lord Christ,
in thee hath it been the good pleasure of God
to sum up all things,
the things in the heavens
and the things upon the earth:
and through thee, through the blood of thy cross,
to reconcile all things unto himself,
whether things upon the earth
or things in the heavens:
that in thy name, Lord Jesus,
every knee should bow,
of things in heaven and things in earth
and things under the earth:
and that every tongue should confess that thou art
Lord,
to the glory of God the Father.

The world needs unity
O Lord, grant that the church may not hinder it, but
promote it, by its own central unity in you.

143. Now unto him that is able to stablish you
according to the eternal gospel of Jesus Christ—
made known unto all the nations,
for their obedience to the faith—
to the only wise God be the glory
for ever and ever. *Amen.*

VI. HIS WITNESSES

36. Apostles

And he went up into the hills, and called to him those whom
he desired; and they came to him.
And he appointed twelve, to be with him, and to be sent out
to preach and have authority to cast out demons.

Mark 3 : 13–14

These twelve Jesus sent out, charging them . . . Preach as
you go, saying, The kingdom of heaven is at hand. Heal
the sick, raise the dead, cleanse lepers, cast out demons.
You received without pay, give without pay. Take no
gold, nor silver, nor copper in your belts, no bag for your
journey, nor two tunics, nor sandals, nor a staff; for the
labourer deserves his food.   *Matthew 10 : 5, 7–10*

And Jesus came and said to them:
All authority in heaven and on earth has been given to
me. Go therefore and make disciples of all nations, baptizing them in the name of the Father and of the Son and of
the Holy Spirit, teaching them to observe all that I have
commanded you; and lo, I am with you always, to the
close of the age.   *Matthew 28 : 18–20*

144. PRAISE BE TO THY NAME for the first disciples who were
sent forth to proclaim the coming of thy kingdom;
for the apostles who, in obedience to thy word,
carried the gospel to many lands;
for the messengers, known and unknown, who
brought the good tidings to our own shores
and for all who have gone to the ends of the world
with the joyful news.
Praise be to thee.

145. O ALMIGHTY GOD, who hast built thy church
upon the foundation of the apostles and prophets,
Jesus Christ himself being the head corner-stone:
Grant us so to be joined together
in unity of spirit by their doctrine,
that we may be made an holy Temple acceptable
unto thee;
through Jesus Christ our Lord.

146. O LORD JESUS CHRIST, who didst send forth thy first
disciples to proclaim thy kingdom, and to teach thy
commandments:
Give to us, thy disciples this day, such an understanding of thy word, that we may teach to others what
we have been taught of thee; to the glory of thy
name, and the spread of thy kingdom.

*Remembering that we can have no share in Christ unless we share in his
mission to the world,*
*let us pray for an ever-deepening sense of mission throughout the whole
church, saying,*

O Christ
I marvel at what you were able to do with ordinary men.
Let me stay with you so that you may make something
usable of me.

147. WE GIVE THANKS TO THEE, O LORD GOD, Father
Almighty, together with thy Son our Lord and
Saviour Jesus Christ, and the Holy Spirit.
All nations offer praise and thanksgiving unto thee, O
Lord, from the rising of the sun unto the going
down thereof, from the north and from the south,
for great is thy name in all nations. *Amen.*

37. Saints and Martyrs

After this I looked, and behold, a great multitude which no man could number, from every nation, from all tribes and peoples and tongues, standing before the throne and before the Lamb, clothed in white robes, with palm branches in their hands, and crying out with a loud voice,

> Salvation belongs to our God who sits upon the throne, and to the Lamb!

And all the angels stood round the throne and round the elders and the four living creatures, and they fell on their faces before the throne and worshipped God, saying,

> Amen! Blessing and glory and wisdom and thanksgiving and honour and power and might be to our God for ever and ever! Amen.

Revelation 7 : 9–12

Therefore, since we are surrounded by so great a cloud of witnesses, let us also lay aside every weight, and sin which clings so closely, and let us run with perseverance the race that is set before us, looking to Jesus the pioneer and perfecter of our faith, who for the joy that was set before him endured the cross, despising the shame, and is seated at the right hand of the throne of God.

Hebrews 12 : 1–2

Let us pray

148. PRAISE BE TO THEE, O GOD,
>>> for the noble army of martyrs all through the ages,
>>> and for all converts to the faith who have sealed
>>>> their witness with their blood;
>>> for the mighty company who now praise thy name,
>>>> out of every kindred and nation and tongue.
>> All praise be to thee, thou king of saints.

149.   ALMIGHTY AND EVERLASTING GOD, who dost enkindle
       the flame of thy love in the hearts of the saints;
       grant to our minds the same faith and power of
       love; that as we rejoice in their triumphs, we may
       profit by their examples; through Jesus Christ our
       Lord.

150.   O KING, ETERNAL, IMMORTAL, INVISIBLE,
           who in the righteousness of thy saints
               hast given us an example of godly life,
           and in their blessedness a glorious pledge
               of the hope of our calling,
       we beseech thee that, being compassed about
           with so great a cloud of witnesses,
       we may run with patience the race that is set before
           us, and with them receive the crown of glory
               that fadeth not away;
           through Jesus Christ our Lord.

151.   ALMIGHTY GOD, by whose grace and power thy holy
                   martyrs
           triumphed over suffering and death:
       Inspire us, we pray thee, with the same faith,
       that, enduring affliction and waxing valiant in fight,
           we with them may secure
               the crown of everlasting life;
           through Jesus Christ our Lord.

*Remembering our Christian brethren throughout the world who are suffering
for their faith, let us say together for them*

O Christ
    let me not fail you in the moment of trial and crisis, which
       is also the moment of opportunity and witness.

152. THE GOD OF ALL GRACE,
who hath called us unto his eternal glory
by Christ Jesus,
after that we have suffered awhile,
make us perfect, stablish, strengthen, settle us,
to him be glory and dominion for ever and ever.
Amen.

38. Everyday Saints

All thy works shall give thanks to thee, O Lord,
    and all thy saints shall bless thee!
They shall speak of the glory of thy kingdom,
    and tell of thy power,
to make known to the sons of men thy mighty deeds,
    and the glorious splendour of thy kingdom.

Psalm 145 : 10–12

Paul, called by the will of God to be an apostle of Christ
    Jesus, and our brother Sosthenes, to the church of God
    which is at Corinth, to those sanctified in Christ Jesus,
    called to be saints together with all those who in every
    place call on the name of our Lord Jesus Christ, both their
    Lord and ours:
Grace to you and peace from God our Father and the Lord
    Jesus Christ.

1 Corinthians 1 : 1–3

Not every one who says to me, Lord, Lord, shall enter the
    kingdom of heaven, but he who does the will of my Father
    who is in heaven.

Matthew 7 : 21

Let us remember
    that to become saints we have only
        to be what God wants us to be
        and to do what God wants us to do;
        to forget ourselves and never to forget God;
    we need
      perfect simplicity with regard to ourselves;
      perfect contentment with all that comes our way;
      perfect peace of mind in utter self-forgetfulness.
    This becomes easier as we realize
      the utter greatness, and goodness,
      and all-ness of God.

153. WE THANK THEE, O GOD, for the saints of all ages;
for those who in times of darkness kept the lamp of
faith burning;
for the great souls who saw visions of larger truth and
dared to declare it;
for the multitude of quiet and gracious souls whose
presence has purified and sanctified the world;
for those known and loved by us, who have passed
from this earthly fellowship into the fuller light of
life with thee;
and for saints in other faiths, who have followed the
truth they knew, and endeavoured to live lives of
virtue and love.

154. O ALMIGHTY GOD, who hast knit together thine elect in
one communion and fellowship, in the mystical
body of thy Son Christ our Lord: Grant us grace so
to follow thy blessed saints in all virtuous and godly
living, that we may come to those unspeakable joys,
which thou hast prepared for them that unfeignedly
love thee; through Jesus Christ our Lord.

155. O LORD, who in every age dost reveal thyself to the
childlike and lowly of heart, and from every race
dost write names in thy book of life:
Give us the simplicity and faith of thy saints, that
loving thee above all things, we may be what thou
wouldst have us be and do what thou wouldst have
us do.
So may we be numbered with thy saints and enter
with them into eternal joy and glory, through Jesus
Christ, our Saviour.

They are known
only to you, O trainer of saints. Fit me to be numbered
among them.

156. GREAT AND MARVELLOUS are thy works, O Lord God,
the Almighty;
righteous and true are thy ways, thou king of saints.
Amen.

39. Ministers of Christ

Our Lord's description of his own ministry
> The Spirit of the Lord is upon me, because he has anointed me to preach good news to the poor.
> He has sent me to proclaim release to the captives and recovering of sight to the blind, to set at liberty those who are oppressed, to proclaim the acceptable year of the Lord.

Luke 4 : 18–19

The Ascended Lord's provision for his church
> But grace was given to each of us according to the measure of Christ's gift . . .
> And his gifts were that some should be apostles, some prophets, some evangelists, some pastors and teachers, for the equipment of the saints, for the work of ministry, for building up the body of Christ,
> until we all attain to the unity of the faith and of the knowledge of the Son of God, to mature manhood, to the measure of the stature of the fullness of Christ.

Ephesians 4 : 7, 11–13

Ministers of the word and sacraments
> So those who received Peter's word were baptized, and there were added that day about three thousand souls.
> And they devoted themselves to the apostles' teaching and fellowship, to the breaking of bread and the prayers.

Acts 2 : 41–42

Let us pray
> for the ministers of all communions,
> of every race and country,
> that they may be holy and humble in heart,
> full of the Spirit, and of wisdom and faith,
> faithful ministers of the word and sacraments;

for all ordained ministers in specialist posts—
    in education, industry, church administration,
    literature production and ecumenical relationships;
that the Holy Spirit may show us the way
    to a ministry which shall be recognized
    throughout the whole church;
that Christians may support their ministers
    by regular prayer and by the expectation
    to receive through them the word of the Lord.

157. ALMIGHTY GOD, the giver of all good gifts,
    who of thy divine providence
    hast appointed divers orders in thy church:
Give thy grace, we humbly beseech thee,
    to all those who are called
    to any office and administration in the same;
and so replenish them with the truth of thy doctrine,
    and endue them with innocency of life,
that they may faithfully serve before thee,
    to the glory of thy great name,
    and the benefit of thy holy church;
through Jesus Christ our Lord.

158. WE PRAY THEE, LORD, for all who minister in thy
    name.
Strengthen them in time of weakness and trial,
    and direct them in all their work.
Give unto them the spirit of power, and of love,
    and of sound mind,
that in all their work they may set forth thy glory,
    and set forward the salvation of souls;
so that the nations may become thine inheritance,
and the uttermost parts of the earth thy possession;
    through Jesus Christ our Lord.

159. GRANT, O GOD, we beseech thee, that the same mind
        may be in all the ministers of thy church,
           that was in Christ Jesus;
                his self-forgetting humility;
                his interest in common things;
                his love for common people;
                his compassion for the fallen;
                his tolerance with the mistaken;
                his patience with the slow;
    and in all their work and converse
    make them continually sensitive to thy guidance
        and ready for thy will,
           through Jesus Christ our Lord.

Let them be
    holy and humble in heart, speaking your word, channel-
    ling your grace and shepherding your people, O shep-
    herd of souls.

160. UNTO HIM that loved us,
        and washed us from our sins, in his own blood,
        and hath made us kings and priests unto God,
           to him be glory and dominion,
                for ever and ever. *Amen.*

40. A Royal Priesthood

Now therefore, if you will obey my voice and keep my covenant, you shall be my own possession among all peoples;
for all the earth is mine, and you shall be to me a kingdom of
priests and a holy nation.

Exodus 19 : 5, 6

You shall be called the priests of the Lord, men shall speak of
you as the ministers of our God.

Isaiah 61 : 6

But you are a chosen race, a royal priesthood, a holy nation,
God's own people, that you may declare the wonderful
deeds of him who called you out of darkness into his marvellous light.

1 Peter 2 : 9

Meditation
These words of scripture are addressed
to all the people of God;
all have their part in worship, in witness,
and in bringing other people to God:
all have a responsibility for others.
The real battles of the faith today are being fought
in factories, shops, offices, and farms,
in political parties and government agencies,
in countless homes,
in the press, radio and television,
in the relationship of nations.
Often it is said that the church should go
into these spheres,
but the fact is that the church is already there
in the persons of its laity.

161. ALMIGHTY AND EVERLASTING GOD,
      by whose Spirit the whole body of the church
        is governed and sanctified:
      Receive our prayers,
          which we offer before thee
      for all members of thy holy church,
        that every one of us
        in our vocation and ministry,
      may in true and godly manner serve thee;
through our Lord and Saviour Jesus Christ.

162. WE COMMEND TO THEE, ALMIGHTY GOD, the whole
Christian church throughout the world.
Bless all in every place who call on the name of our
Lord Jesus Christ.
May the grace and power of the Holy Spirit fill every
member, so that all the company of thy faithful
people may bear witness for thee on the earth.
Look in mercy on the errors and confusions of our
time, and draw the hearts of believers nearer to the
Lord Jesus Christ.
If it be good in thy sight, heal the outward divisions of
thy people, disposing the wills of all to a true union
of order in the truth, for the work of the one Lord.
And above all we pray for the unity of the Spirit,
through whom alone we are guided into all truth.

163. HERE, O LORD, WE OFFER and present unto thee
      ourselves, our souls and bodies,
    to be a reasonable, holy and living sacrifice;
      humbly beseeching thee
     that thou wilt accept this our offering,
     and use it for the work of thy kingdom,
  and the making known of thy love to all mankind;
    through Jesus Christ our Lord.

164. LOOK DOWN, O LORD, upon our fellow Christians
who are scattered abroad,
and quicken in them the fire of thy love,
that realizing the blessedness of the true faith,
they may become living witnesses for thee,
in word and deed,
unto the people amongst whom they dwell;
who livest and reignest
with the Father and the Holy Spirit,
one God for ever and ever.

Let us pray especially for the lay people
who serve God in many kinds of church work:
elders and deacons, churchwardens and treasurers,
women workers, Sunday school teachers,
secretaries, sidesmen, vergers,
choir members, organists and many others.

Every one of us
is called, dear Master, to assist in your saving ministry and
the struggle for your kingdom.

165. GO FORTH INTO THE WORLD in peace;
be of good courage; hold fast that which is good;
render to no man evil for evil;
strengthen the fainthearted;
support the weak, help the afflicted;
honour all men;
love and serve the Lord,
rejoicing in the power of the Holy Spirit.
And the blessing of God Almighty,
the Father, the Son, and the Holy Spirit,
be upon you
and remain with you for ever. *Amen.*

41. Religious Communities

Blessed are they that dwell in thy house:
    they will be always praising thee.
Blessed is the man whose strength is in thee,
    in whose heart are thy ways;
who going through the vale of misery use it for a well,
    and the pools are filled with water.
They will go from strength to strength,
and unto the God of gods appeareth every one of
      them in Zion.

Psalm 84 : 4–7

Now the company of those who believed were of one heart
    and soul, and no one said that any of the things which he
    possessed was his own, but they had everything in com-
    mon.

Acts 4 : 32

How lovely is thy dwelling place, O Lord of hosts!
My soul longs, yea, faints for the courts of the Lord;
    my heart and flesh sing for joy
    to the living God . . .
For a day in thy courts is better than a thousand . . .

Psalm 84 : 1, 2, 10

O God, thou art my God, early will I seek thee.
My soul thirsteth for thee, my flesh also longeth after thee in
    a barren and dry land where no water is.
Thus have I looked for thee in holiness,
    that I might behold thy power and glory;
For thy lovingkindness is better than the life itself,
    my lips shall praise thee.

Psalm 63 : 1–3

Let us thank God
> for all who have sacrificed the joys of family life that they
> may serve God in religious communities
> for their discipline of worship and practice of contem-
> plative prayer
> for their concern for the world and their engagement in
> intercession
> for the growing interest in contemplative prayer
> for the stimulation to meditation that comes from the
> methods practised by people in other faiths.

Let us pray
> that members of our churches may be ready to accept the
> help of the religious communities in deepening their
> spiritual life
> for God's blessing on the worship and work of the religious
> communities
> that they may be guided by the Holy Spirit to find ways of
> helping our generation to quiet waiting upon God, to
> stillness of mind, and a more intimate and personal
> knowledge of God.

166. FATHER, SON AND HOLY SPIRIT
subdue the turmoil of my heart
that in the unifying calm of love
where thought is hushed to rest
all may be stilled for loving intercourse
with thee.
Make me so to dwell with thee
that I may forget myself
and be of one soul with thee
my well-beloved Lord.

167. INCREASE, O LORD, the number who are called to
seek and give both time and quietude for the work of
prayer and penitence in this age of dark confusion.

168. O GOD who art the exceeding great reward
         of those who seek thee,
      prosper the endeavours of those whom thou hast
            called
      to devote themselves entirely to thy worship:
      cherish and guide them by the inspiration
         of thy Holy Spirit,
            that they may be truly centred upon thee,
      and worship thee in sincerity and truth;
            through Jesus Christ our Lord.

O God
   I thank you for men and women who dedicate their lives
      to worship and contemplation, holding the world before
      you for love, sanctification and blessing.

42. Training for the Ministry

In the year that King Uzziah died I saw the Lord sitting
　upon a throne, high and lifted up;
　and his train filled the temple.
Above him stood the seraphim; each had six wings:
　with two he covered his face, and with two he covered
　his feet, and with two he flew.
　And one called to another and said:
　　Holy, holy, holy is the Lord of hosts;
　　the whole earth is full of his glory.
And the foundations of the thresholds shook at the voice of
　him who called, and the house was filled with smoke.
And I said: Woe is me! For I am lost; for I am a man of
　unclean lips, and I dwell in the midst of a people of
　unclean lips;
　for my eyes have seen the king, the Lord of hosts!
Then flew one of the seraphim to me,
　having in his hand a burning coal which he had taken
　with tongs from the altar. And he touched my mouth, and
　said:
　　Behold, this has touched your lips;
　　your guilt is taken away, and your sin forgiven.
And I heard the voice of the Lord saying,
　　Whom shall I send, and who will go for us?
Then I said, Here I am! Send me.

Isaiah 6 : 1–8

When he saw the crowds, he had compassion for them,
　because they were harassed and helpless, like sheep with-
　out a shepherd.
Then he said to his disciples,
　　The harvest is plentiful, but the labourers are few; pray
　　therefore the Lord of the harvest to send out labourers
　　into his harvest.

Matthew 9 : 36–38

But you, beloved, build yourselves up on your most holy
    faith;
pray in the Holy Spirit;
keep yourselves in the love of God;
wait for the mercy of our Lord Jesus Christ unto eternal life.

Jude 20–21

Let us pray
    for the men and women who are being trained for the
        ministry of the church in our own country and in other
        countries;
    for the guidance of the Holy Spirit in all plans for the
        deepening and developing of theological training;
    that the necessary books for training the ministry may be
        made available in all languages;
    that the Holy Spirit may guide the church in calling and
        training a voluntary ministry to assist the whole-time
        ministers, so that every Christian group may have an
        adequate ministry of both word and sacrament.

169. WE PRAY, O LORD, for thy blessing
            upon all who are being trained
            for the ministry of thy church in every land.
        Take from them all pride and self-conceit,
            all thought of worldly advancement.
        May their wills be wholly surrendered unto thee;
        fill them with thy Spirit, that they may go forth
            inspired with zeal for thy glory and a love of souls,
            in the power of our Lord Jesus Christ.

170. O ALMIGHTY GOD, look mercifully upon the world
            which thou hast redeemed
            by the blood of thy dear Son,
        and incline the hearts of many to offer themselves
            for the sacred ministry of thy church;

119

so that by their labours
thy light may shine in the darkness,
and the coming of thy kingdom may be hastened
by the perfecting of thine elect;
through the same Jesus Christ our Lord.

A prayer for theological colleges

171. O EVERLASTING GOD, adored and served by the hosts
of heaven yet choosing to use men upon earth to
lead the praises of thy creatures and to bestow upon
thy people mercy and forgiveness:
Graciously pour we pray thee thy blessing upon
theological colleges;
Preserve and renew the customs and teaching given
and observed therein, that they who are there to
learn and be trained may by thee be strengthened
in loyalty and love, disciplined and nurtured by thy
word and sacraments,
and when the time is come, being ordained ministers
of the new covenant, go forth into the world and
advance thy glory and the welfare of thy children;
through thine eternally begotten and beloved Son,
Jesus Christ our Lord and Saviour.

We need, dear Lord
a ministerial succession, confident in your grace, flexible in
your hands, unfailing in your love.

172. TEACH US, GOOD LORD, to serve thee as thou deservest;
to give and not to count the cost;
to fight and not to heed the wounds;
to toil and not to seek for rest;
to labour and to ask for no reward,
save that of knowing that we do thy will;
through Jesus Christ our Lord. *Amen.*

VII. HIS KINGDOM

43. Our citizenship is in Heaven

Our commonwealth is in heaven, and from it we await a
Saviour, the Lord Jesus Christ, who will change our lowly
body to be like his glorious body, by the power which
enables him even to subject all things to himself.

Philippians 3 : 20–21

If then you have been raised with Christ, seek the things that
are above, where Christ is, seated at the right hand of
God.
Set your minds on things that are above, not on things that
are on earth. For you have died, and your life is hid with
Christ in God.
When Christ who is our life appears, then you also will
appear with him in glory.

Colossians 3 : 1–4

By faith Abraham sojourned in the land of promise . . .
For he looked forward to the city which has foundations,
whose builder and maker is God.

Hebrews 11 : 9–10

An ancient act of faith
173.   THE LORD is my shepherd, therefore can I lack
nothing.
He shall feed me in a green pasture,
and lead me forth beside the waters of comfort.
He shall convert my soul, and bring me forth
in the paths of righteousness, for his name's sake.
Yea, though I walk through the valley of the
shadow of death,
I will fear no evil, for thou art with me . . .
I will dwell in the house of the Lord for ever.

174. O GOD, THE PROTECTOR of all that trust in thee,
without whom nothing is strong, nothing is holy:
Increase and multiply upon us thy mercy;
that, thou being our ruler and guide,
we may so pass through things temporal,
that we lose not the things eternal:
Grant this, O heavenly Father,
for Jesus Christ's sake our Lord.

175. O GOD, WHO RULEST the world from everlasting to
everlasting:
Speak to our hearts when courage fails,
and we faint for fear;
when our love grows cold,
and there is distress of nations upon the earth.
Keep us resolute and steadfast in the things
that cannot be shaken,
abounding in hope
and knowing that our labour is not in vain in thee.

Let us pray for justice and peace
176. ALMIGHTY GOD, our heavenly Father, guide, we
beseech thee, the nations of the world into the way
of justice and truth, and establish among them that
peace which is the fruit of righteousness, through
Jesus Christ, the prince of peace.

Keep our eyes, O Lord
on the real and the eternal, the centre of initiative, the
powerhouse of grace, and the home of the human spirit.

177. MAY THE ETERNAL GOD BLESS and keep us,
guard our bodies, save our souls, direct our thoughts,
and bring us safe to the heavenly country, our eternal
home,
where Father, Son and Holy Spirit ever reign,
one God for ever and ever. *Amen.*

44. Power

Power is delegated from God
All the whole heavens are the Lord's: the earth has he given to the children of men.

Psalm 115 : 16 (B.C.P.)

Thou hast given him dominion over the works of thy hands; thou hast put all things under his feet.

Psalm 8 : 6

Our God has spoken; twice have I heard this: that power belongs to God.

Psalm 62 : 11

Let us reflect
that in the kingdom of God, power is always used in the motive of love
that those in power are answerable to God and to their own people
that citizens can take their part in informed criticism of their governments and in many countries choose those governments
that love is the greatest power of all
that nations and governments are sensitive to world opinion
that democracy is not just the vote of the majority but decision paying regard to the rights and needs of the minority also.

For the right use of power
178. ALMIGHTY AND MERCIFUL GOD, without whom all things hasten to destruction and fall into nothingness: Look, we beseech thee, upon thy family of nations and men, to which thou hast committed power in trust for their mutual health and comfort.

Save us and help us, O Lord, lest we abuse thy gift
and make it our misery and ruin; draw all men unto
thee in thy kingdom of righteousness and truth;
uproot our enmities, heal our divisions, cast out our
fears; and renew our faith in thine unchanging purpose of goodwill and peace on earth; for the love of
Jesus Christ our Lord.

For delivery from fears about power

179. O GOD, save us from fear, the fear of the weak of those
who have power and the fear of those who have
power that they should lose it. Grant also that all
who have power may use it in subordination to love
and the welfare of all over whom they have power.
We ask this as citizens of thy kingdom and followers
of thy Son Jesus Christ, our Lord.

When we are powerless

180. O GOD, whose blessed Son was powerless in the hands
of men and did not fail in love to all who had a
hand in his death: grant that when we have no
power, we may exercise the power of love and pray
that the righteous and loving will be done, as it was
by thy Son, our Lord Jesus Christ.

Let me repeat

again and again, O God, that thine is the kingdom, the
power and the glory, for ever and ever. Amen! Amen!

181. Worthy art thou to take the scroll
           and to open its seals,
      for thou wast slain and by thy blood didst ransom
           men for God
      from every tribe and tongue and people and nation,
      and hast made them a kingdom and priests to our God
      and they shall reign on earth.

45. Christ in Industry

Is not this the carpenter? *Mark 6 : 3*

Who serves as a soldier at his own expense? Who plants a
vineyard without eating any of its fruit? Who tends a flock
without getting some of the milk?
Do I say this on human authority? Does not the law say the
same? For it is written in the law of Moses,
> You shall not muzzle an ox when it is treading out the
> grain.
Is it for oxen that God is concerned? Does he not speak
entirely for our sake? It was written for our sake, because
the plowman should plow in hope and the thresher thresh
in hope of a share in the crop.

1 Corinthians 9 : 7–10

I rejoice in the Lord greatly that now at length you have
revived your concern for me ... Not that I complain of
want; for I have learned, in whatever state I am, to be
content.

Philippians 4 : 10–11

Let us recall with penitence the small part the church in the
west has taken in the social and industrial changes of the
last two hundred years, and the weak impact which the
church makes upon the industrial world today.
Let us thank God for the prophets and reformers who have
revealed spiritual issues and struggled to improve condi-
tions and for dedicated people in industry today, who
strive for right relationships, true values and just condi-
tions.

*Remembering the rapid growth in industry which is taking place all over the
world, and especially in Asia and Africa, let us pray*

for a spirit of service to the community in all involved in
ownership, management and labour;

125

for a deeper valuation of human relationships in industry,
    and a new realization of the importance of family life;
for Christians in industry, that through them the justice and
    love of God may find entry into industrial concerns;
for God's blessing on experiments in partnership, profit-
    sharing, and planning to meet difficulties;
for God's blessing on pastoral and evangelistic experiments,
    especially on industrial chaplains, and priest-workmen.
May Christ be acknowledged as the Lord of all life!

182.   O Lord our God, king of life,
           as we take our place in the working-day world,
              with its cares and labours,
              with its temptations,
           help us to serve thee in all that we do.
           Lead us in the right path.
           Grant us to walk in safety.
           Teach us to do what is for our salvation.
     In the name of Jesus, thy Son, our Lord and Saviour.

183.   Jesus, the Master Carpenter, who at the last
           through wood and nails purchased man's whole sal-
           vation: Wield well thy tools in this workshop of
           thine, that we who come rough-hewn may here be
           fashioned to a truer beauty by thy hand.

184.   O Lord, make thy way plain before us;
           let thy glory be our end,
              thy word our rule;
           and as always, thy will be done. *Amen.*

Our Father's business
    dear Lord, is all honest work, carried out in fellowship,
        with due regard for the rights and needs of all classes in
        the community.

46. Nations United

The vision of the prophets reflects the desire of the people of all nations

It shall come to pass in the latter days that the mountain
of the house of the Lord shall be established as the
highest of the mountains, and shall be raised up above
the hills; and peoples shall flow to it, and many nations
shall come, and say:
> Come, let us go up to the mountain of the Lord, to
> the house of the God of Jacob; that he may teach
> us his ways and we may walk in his paths.

For out of Zion shall go forth the law, and the word of the
Lord from Jerusalem. He shall judge between many
peoples, and shall decide for strong nations afar off; and
they shall beat their swords into plowshares, and their
spears into pruning hooks;
nation shall not lift up sword against nation, neither shall
they learn war any more.

Micah 4 : 1–3

The wilderness and the solitary place shall be glad; and the
desert shall rejoice, and blossom as the rose . . .
Then the eyes of the blind shall be opened, and the ears of
the deaf shall be unstopped.
Then shall the lame man leap as an hart, and the tongue of
the dumb shall sing: for in the wilderness shall waters
break out, and streams in the desert.

Isaiah 35 : 1, 5, 6 (R.V.)

Thus says the Lord of hosts:
> Old men and old women shall again sit in the streets of
> Jerusalem, each with staff in hand for very age. And the
> streets of the city shall be full of boys and girls playing in
> its streets.

Zechariah 8 : 4, 5

    that the leaders of the nations now meet together round
the conference table to deal with problems of world
peace, to correct injustices and to discuss grievances;

for the growing acceptance of a common standard of
human rights and freedom for all peoples and all
nations;

for the sharing of knowledge and art and culture, for the
mutual inspiration and example in education by means
of the United Nations Educational, Scientific and
Cultural Organization;

for the sharing of medical science, the rescue work in
emergency and epidemic, the efforts to banish widespread disease, undertaken by the World Health
Organization;

for the joint consultation in the Food and Agriculture
Organization in its efforts to preserve the fertility of the
earth, fight pests, increase food production and distrib-
ute supplies more equally;

for the care for homeless refugees and the relief for war-
stricken people, given through the United Nations
Refugee Emergency Fund.

185. ALMIGHTY GOD, OUR HEAVENLY FATHER,
        guide we beseech thee the nations of the world into
        the way of justice and truth
        and establish among them that peace
          which is the fruit of righteousness.

186. O HEAVENLY FATHER, we thank thee for those who out
        of the bitter memories of strife and loss
          are seeking a more excellent way
          for the nations of the world,
        whereby justice and order may be maintained
        and the differences of peoples be resolved in equity.
    We pray thee to establish their purpose on sure
          foundations
          and to prosper their labours, that thy will
          may be done;
        for the sake of Jesus Christ our Lord.

187. LORD OF THE NATIONS, Creator, Redeemer and Father of all men, we thank thee for the vision of thy purpose to gather all nations into a commonwealth of justice, peace and brotherhood. We thank thee for the United Nations Organization with its aim to avoid war, with its service in production of food, its promotion of education and health, its care of refugees and children. Encourage us to learn more about other people and their needs, so that we may love and serve them better. Guide all the nations and their leaders, we pray thee, into deeper unity, greater efforts for peace, more generous contributions to human welfare, that men may live free from fear and free from want, and help build the universe of thy love, made known to us in Jesus Christ, our Lord.

188. ALL THE ENDS of the earth shall remember and turn unto the Lord, and all the kindreds of the nations shall worship before thee. For the kingdom is the Lord's; and he is the ruler over the nations. *Amen.*

Grant, O God
that the second great commandment of your Law may govern all our social and national relationships as well as our personal lives.

47. The Christian Home

The child Jesus at Nazareth
And the child grew and became strong, filled with wisdom; and the favour of God was upon him . . .
And he went down with them [Mary and Joseph] and came to Nazareth, and was obedient to them . . .

Luke 2 : 40, 51

Jesus speaks of the divine institution of marriage
From the beginning of creation, God made them male and female. For this reason a man shall leave his father and mother and be joined to his wife, and the two shall become one . . .
What therefore God has joined together, let not man put asunder.

Mark 10 : 6–9

A whole family is baptized
One who heard us was a woman named Lydia, from the city of Thyatira, a seller of purple goods, who was a worshipper of God. The Lord opened her heart to give heed to what was said by Paul.
And when she was baptized, with her household, she besought us, saying, If you have judged me to be faithful to the Lord, come to my house and stay.

Acts 16 : 14, 15

Paul greets a Christian household
Paul, a prisoner for Christ Jesus, and Timothy our brother, to Philemon our beloved fellow worker and Apphia our sister and Archippus our fellow soldier, and the church in your house:
Grace to you and peace from God our Father and the Lord Jesus Christ.

Philemon: 1–3

Let us thank God
 for the divine institution of family life with its mutual love
  and caring, its joy and support in trouble;
 that our Lord Jesus Christ shared the life of an earthly
  home, was obedient to Mary and Joseph, was ready to
  leave his home at God's call, and when dying on the
  cross made provision for his mother;
 for all that Christ and his church mean to us in our family
  life;
 for the witness to others of the Christian home;
 for the continuing Jewish emphasis on family life.

Let us pray
 that God's plan of family life may be understood and
  accepted in all parts of the world;
 that there may be a return in the west to Christian stan-
  dards of faithfulness in marriage;
 that in other parts polygamy may be abandoned and a
  deep spiritual and lifelong ideal of marriage be accepted;
 for broken homes, that the love of God may redeem and
  re-make;
 for the Refugee Service of the World Council of Churches
  and for all who are seeking to help the homeless.

189. LORD GOD ALMIGHTY, FATHER OF EVERY FAMILY,
  against whom no door can be shut;
  Enter all homes, we beseech thee, with the angel of
   thy presence, to hallow them in pureness and
   beauty of love;
  and by thy dear Son, born in a stable, move our
   hearts to hear the cry of the homeless, and to
   convert all sordid and bitter dwellings into house-
   holds of thine;
  through Jesus Christ our Lord.

190. O God our Father, in whom all the families of the earth are blessed: We pray thee to regard with thy lovingkindness the homes of our country; that marriage may be held in due honour by the church, by the state, and by society; and that husbands and wives may live faithfully together, in honour preferring one another. We pray that the members of every family may be rich in mutual understanding and forbearance, in courtesy and kindness, bearing one another's burdens, and so fulfilling the law of Christ, thy Son, our Lord.

191. Heavenly Father,
from whom all fatherhood in heaven and
earth is named:
Bless, we beseech thee, all children,
and give to their parents,
and to all in whose charge they may be,
thy spirit of wisdom and love;
so that the home in which they grow up
may be to them an image of thy kingdom,
and the care of their parents a likeness of thy love.

192. O Lord Jesus Christ, who on the cross didst
remember
thy Mother and thy friend,
make our homes to be homes of love.
Spread thy grace over every relationship of human
life,
so that all our earthly love
may be gathered up into the love of God,
and thy kingdom made manifest to men
in the homes of thy people.

We need a place, O Father
   which we can remember with grateful love, return to for
   rest after work, support in trouble, encouragement in
   the adventure of life, patterned on the heavenly
   Nazareth.

193.   WE BOW OUR KNEES UNTO THE FATHER,
            from whom every family in heaven and in
            earth is named.

48. The Kingdom of His Christ

In the kingdom of God uncompromising obedience to God is essential
  Again, the devil took him to a very high mountain, and
  showed him all the kingdoms of the world and the glory
  of them; and he said to him,
        All these I will give you, if you will fall down and
        worship me.
  Then Jesus said to him,
        Begone, Satan! for it is written, You shall worship the
        Lord your God and him only shall you serve.

Matthew 4 : 8–10

Spiritual principles are prior to material things
  Seek first his kingdom and his righteousness, and all these
  things shall be yours as well.

Matthew 6 : 33

Humble service is the highest qualification
  Whoever would be great among you must be your servant
  and whoever would be first among you must be slave of
  all.

Mark 10 : 44

  Let us pray that God may bless and uphold our brethren
in countries where true religion is oppressed and restricted
today, keeping them faithful, and sanctifying their witness.

194.   O GOD, THE KING OF RIGHTEOUSNESS, leads us,
              we pray thee,
           in ways of justice and peace:
           inspire us to break down all tyranny and
              oppression,
           to gain for every man his due reward,
           and from every man his due service;
        that each may live for all and all may care for each, in
           Jesus Christ our Lord.

195. O GOD OF JUSTICE AND LOVE, forgive us and our fore-
fathers that we have been so lukewarm in working
for thy kingdom. Forgive thy church in that the
dispossessed of all nations have not seen in it the
hope of a new order and the promise of human
brotherhood and world peace.
Cleanse and renew us, and teach us to put thy kingdom before every other loyalty and thy will before
every desire, through Jesus Christ our Lord.

196. O THOU WHO ART THE LIGHT of the world,
the desire of all nations,
and the shepherd of our souls:
let thy light shine in the darkness,
and by the lifting up of thy cross
gather the peoples unto thee,
that all the ends of the earth may see
the salvation of God.

197. O CHRIST, who in thyself art both the gospel and the
kingdom,
show us how to preach good news
to those who fight for the kingdom of this world.
Help us to proclaim thy love for them
and call them in to work for the new heaven and earth
which comes down from heaven,
so that both they and we may rejoice in thy kingdom
of righteousness, peace and joy, which has no end,
and worship the God who never fails,
even our Creator and Saviour, blessed for evermore.
Amen.

How slowly, O Lord
the kingdom comes, at our pace rather than at yours. O
God, I want it for the world and myself. Show me how
to work for it and how to combine with others to hasten
its coming.

49. The Christian Warfare

Paul shows us the character of our warfare
Though we live in the world we are not carrying on a worldly war, for the weapons of our warfare are not worldly but have divine power to destroy strongholds. We destroy arguments and every proud obstacle to the knowledge of God, and take every thought captive to obey Christ.

2 Corinthians 10 : 3–5

He enumerates our spiritual weapons
Finally, be strong in the Lord and in the strength of his might. Put on the whole armour of God, that you may be able to stand against the wiles of the devil.

For we are not contending against flesh and blood, but against the principalities, against the powers, against the world rulers of this present darkness, against the spiritual hosts of wickedness in the heavenly places.

Therefore take the whole armour of God, that you may be able to withstand in the evil day, and having done all, to stand.

Stand therefore, having girded your loins with truth, and having put on the breastplate of righteousness, and having shod your feet with the equipment of the gospel of peace; above all taking the shield of faith, with which you can quench all the flaming darts of the evil one.

Ephesians 6 : 10–16

Meditation
Let us remember our Lord healing an enemy at his arrest, mocked in the guardroom yet undefeated in love, on the cross praying for those who nailed him there.

Let us meditate on the only weapons Christians may use, praying that evil may never defeat us into retaliation, but that we may overcome evil with good, and win men by love and truth.

198. O LORD GOD, keep ever in our remembrance
        the life and death of our Saviour Jesus Christ.
      Make the thought of his love powerful to win us from
          evil.
      As he toiled and sorrowed and suffered for us,
          in fighting against sin,
      so may we endure constantly and labour diligently,
          as his soldiers and servants,
          looking ever unto him
      and counting it all joy to be partakers with him
      in his conflict, his cross and his victory.

199. ETERNAL GOD, in whose perfect kingdom
          no sword is drawn but the sword of righteousness,
          and no strength known but the strength of love:
      help thy soldiers to fight the good fight of faith,
          refusing the weapons of the devil and the world,
          and overcoming hatred with love, evil with
              goodness, falsehood with truth,
          and so extending the victory of the cross;
              through him who triumphed thereon,
          even thy Son, our Saviour Jesus Christ.

200. LORD JESUS, who wast silent when men nailed thee to
      the cross, and by pain didst triumph over pain:
      Pour thy spirit, we beseech thee, on thy servants
      when they suffer, that in their quietness and cour-
      age thou mayest triumph again; who livest and
      reignest in the glory of the eternal Trinity, God,
      world without end.

Disarm me, O Christ
    of aggressiveness, hatred, self-seeking, and let me fight only
    with the weapons of truth, goodness and love.

201. THE PEACE OF GOD
          which passeth all understanding
          guard our hearts and thoughts
          in Christ Jesus. *Amen.*

137

VIII. THE ENDS OF THE EARTH

50. A Light to the Nations

The first worshippers from the nations

Now when Jesus was born in Bethlehem of Judea in the
days of Herod the king, behold, wise men from the east
came to Jerusalem, saying,
Where is he who has been born king of the Jews?
For we have seen his star in the east, and have come to
worship him . . .

and going into the house they saw the child with Mary his
mother, and they fell down and worshipped him. Then,
opening their treasures, they offered him gifts, gold and
frankincense and myrrh.

Matthew 2 : 1, 2, 11

Paul sees that salvation is for all nations

The mystery was made known to me by revelation . . .
that is, how the Gentiles are fellow heirs, members of
the same body, and partakers of the promise in Christ
Jesus through the gospel . . .
To me, though I am the very least of all the saints, this
grace was given, to preach to the Gentiles the unsearchable riches of Christ.

Ephesians 3 : 3, 6, 8

In the worship of the wise men let us see the promise that all
nations shall come and worship thee, O Lord.
In the founding of the church in every land let us see the
fulfilment of the promise of the Epiphany.

202. ALMIGHTY AND EVERLASTING GOD, the brightness of faithful souls, who didst bring the Gentiles to thy light and make known unto them him who is the true light, and the bright and morning star:
Fill, we beseech thee, the world with thy glory, and show thyself by the radiance of thy light unto all nations; through Jesus Christ our Lord.

203. LORD JESUS CHRIST, who in the offerings of the wise men didst receive an earnest of the worship of the nations:
Grant that thy church may never cease to proclaim the good news of thy love, that all men may come to worship thee as their Saviour and king, who livest and reignest world without end.

204. LORD OF THE HARVEST, the nations are waiting for thy message, and asking for messengers, and there are few who go, and few who give, and few who pray.
O grant that we may hear thy voice, and help in whatever way we can, by prayer, by gifts, and by service, to make thy gospel known to all the world; for the sake of Jesus Christ our Saviour.

In the face of Jesus Christ
I see your smile, O hidden God, and know that it welcomes and gladdens the hearts of people everywhere, like the sunrise.

205. GOD BE MERCIFUL unto us, and bless us, and shew us the light of his countenance, and be merciful unto us;
that thy way may be known upon earth, thy saving health among all nations . . .
Let the people praise thee, O God; yea, let all the people praise thee.
Then shall the earth bring forth her increase, and God, even our own God, shall give us his blessing.

51. Every Nation

God's covenant with the whole of mankind
> When the bow is in the cloud, I will look upon it and
> remember the everlasting covenant between God and
> every living creature of all flesh that is upon the earth.
>
> *Genesis 9 : 16*

All nations to receive a blessing
> And I will make of you a great nation, and I will bless
> you, and make your name great, so that you will be a
> blessing . . . and by you all the families of the earth shall
> bless themselves. *Genesis 12 : 2–3*

Saints from every nation
> After this I looked, and behold, a great multitude which
> no man could number, from every nation, from all
> tribes and peoples and tongues, standing before the
> throne and before the lamb, clothed in white robes, with
> palm branches in their hands. *Revelation 7 : 9*

Streaming into the city of God
> By its light shall the nations walk; and the kings of the
> earth shall bring their glory into it, and its gates shall
> never be shut by day—and there shall be no night there.
>
> *Revelation 21 : 24–25*

Each in its own culture
206. O Lord Jesus Christ, who didst grow up within the
culture of thine own people: Grant that each race
may worship God in its own tradition, respecting
the ways of other races so that in varying forms, as
in differing languages, people may offer their devotion and praise to the Creator, Father and inspirer
of all, blessed in his many names, now and always.

An Indian prayer
207. Lord Jesus Christ, help us to discover your hidden
presence in the living traditions of our country, so

that we too may be led by this discovery from the unreality of our narrow views to the reality of your infinite presence; from the darkness of our ignorance of your ways to the light of your full revelation; and from the depth of our sinful self-sufficiency to the immortal life of your love.

A Bantu prayer

208.   We offer our thanks to thee
        for sending thy only Son to die for us all.
  In a world suffocated with colour bars,
      how sweet a thing it is to know
      that in thee we all belong to one family.
  There are times when we,
        unprivileged people,
      weep tears that are not loud but deep,
      when we think of the suffering we experience.
  We come to thee, our only hope and refuge.
  Help us, O God, to refuse to be embittered
      against those who handle us with harshness.
      We are grateful to thee
      for the gift of laughter at all times.
  Save us from hatred of those who oppress us.
  May we follow the spirit of thy Son Jesus Christ.

An Australian prayer

209.   O LOVING FATHER, from this fair land under southern skies we lift up our hearts in praise to thee for thy great goodness to us as a people; for those brave souls who, sailing unknown seas, found here a wealth of beauty and of opportunity; for those stout-hearted pioneers who, undaunted by difficulties and defeats, crossed the ranges, and in this land of wide horizons, built their homes and laid the foundations of a new order of life. Grant us the vision of thy purpose for this nation and of thy saving love for all mankind, through Jesus Christ our Lord.

In your providence, O God
   We hope for a new covenant with every nation, that all
   may be thy people and enjoy thy saving love.

All nations whom thou hast made shall bow down before
   thee, O Lord, and shall glorify thy name. For thou art
   great and doest wondrous things; thou alone art God.

Psalm 86 : 9

52. God at Work in Others

God always at work everywhere
In many and various ways God spoke of old to our fathers
by the prophets; but in these last days he has spoken to
us by a Son, whom he appointed the heir of all things,
through whom also he created the world.

Hebrews 1 : 1–2

The divine light always shining
The true light that enlightens every man was coming into
the world.

John 1 : 9

God moves in the hearts of others
And the people of Nineveh believed God: they proclaimed
a fast, and put on sackcloth, from the greatest of them to
the least of them ... But it displeased Jonah exceed-
ingly.

Jonah 3 : 5

Others share in God's saving providence
Melchizedek, King of Salem, priest of God most high
blesses Abraham (*Genesis 14 : 19*); Jethro, priest of
Midian befriends and advises Moses (*Exodus 18 : 1–12*);
Balaam, a Gentile prophet knows the heart of prophecy
(*Numbers 22 : 35*); Ruth the Moabitess becomes the great
grandmother of David (*Matthew 1 : 5*); Job, the man of
Uz, talks with God and hears God's reply (*Job 42 : 5*);
Isaiah speaks of Cyrus as God's Anointed (*Isaiah 45 : 2*).

Others are welcome
I tell you, many will come from east and west and sit at
table with Abraham, Isaac and Jacob in the kingdom of
heaven.

Matthew 8 : 11

Let us reflect

how people everywhere want to discover the meaning of life and death

how people give many different names to God—Ultimate Reality, the Eternal, Divine Wisdom, Divine Light, Brahman, Param-atman, Dhamma, Nirvana, Allah, Tao, Father, the many names in African religions

how the Christian church in its mission to the world has discovered other expressions of faith and forms of worship,

and has shared with people everywhere its own faith that the eternal God revealed himself and his saving love in Jesus Christ.

210. PERSONAL ENCOUNTER

O Spirit of God, guide me
as I seek to discover thy working
with men of other faiths.
Give me the strength of truth,
the gentleness and strength of love,
the clear eye of judgement, and the courage of faith.
Above all, grant me a deeper understanding
of him who is the truth,
a greater commitment to him who is the Lord,
a deeper gratitude to him
who is the Saviour of all,
even Jesus Christ thy eternal Word,
through whom thou art drawing all men
to thyself, that they may be saved for ever,
and worship thee the only God
blessed for evermore.

211. O GOD, I gaze in wonder at thy creative love, at thy seeking for people everywhere and their search for thee, showing thyself in ways they can understand. Help me to learn more of thee from the experience of other communities of faith, and so to live and

love that others may learn to share what I have found of thee in Jesus Christ. Open my eyes, enlighten my mind, enlarge my heart, and grant that my own expression of thee in life and word may come closer to thy eternal truth and love. O God, my God, God of all.

212. CHRIST ON EVERY ROAD
O Christ, my way
   to the God of all salvation,
men of other faiths
   believe they have their own salvation faith.
Be with them, dear Lord,
   to encourage them on their way
   to their own Jerusalem
so that we all find ourselves
   with the spirits of just men made perfect
   with the saints of every age and faith
in the presence of the eternal God
   the God of many names,
Creator, lover, Saviour of us all.

Let me see, O God
  the colours of the spiritual rainbow, each lovely, and all
    making up the pure light of your presence.

53. All God's People

All God's People
> In that day Israel will be the third with Egypt and Assyria, a blessing in the midst of the earth, whom the Lord of hosts has blessed, saying, Blessed be Egypt my people, and Assyria the work of my hands, and Israel my heritage.
>
> *Isaiah 19 : 24–25*

Other sheep in other folds
> And I have other sheep, that are not of this fold; I must bring them also, and they will heed my voice. So there shall be one flock, one shepherd.
>
> *John 10 : 16*

A great day ahead
> And the Lord will become king over all the earth; on that day the Lord will be one and his name one.
>
> *Zechariah 14 : 9*

A warning for all
> But we have this treasure in earthen vessels to show that the transcendent power belongs to God and not to us.
>
> *2 Corinthians 4 : 7*

Let us reflect
> how through the mission of the church we have discovered that all people have some knowledge of God, glimpses of truth, desire for salvation, practice of meditation and prayer, teaching about the good life, some hope of life after death
>
> that in our growing knowledge of the founders and saints of other faiths we see that God has never left himself without witness
>
> that we are on holy ground when we consider the heart of other religions, their central affirmation and what they conceive to be their mission and their gospel

that one result of the church's mission has been stimulation
and revival of other faiths

that people of different faiths are now explaining themselves to one another, listening to one another, learning
from one another, wondering if they can begin to work
together for human welfare, social justice and world
peace

that we all need God's truth, God's love, God's grace in
our own discipleships and interpretation of our experience of him.

Thanksgivings

For the Buddha

213. O GOD, who art the Creator of all worlds
and the Lord of all ages,
I praise thee for the Buddha
who taught men that desire, greed, and attachment
were the causes of men's misery.
I thank thee for his teaching
of the noble eightfold path
which men should tread
and for his compassion for all that has life.
Grant that those who follow him as teacher
may find his wisdom confirmed
in thy Word Jesus Christ,
through whom they may receive forgiveness
and saving grace,
strength to live the good life,
and finally by thy mercy
the enjoyment of eternal life in thy heaven,
through the same Jesus Christ our Lord.

For Muhammad

214. O GOD, I thank thee for Muhammad and for his
Muslim followers who assert thy transcendence, thy
sovereignty and thy uniqueness. Grant that
Christians and Muslims may speak to each other
from their experience of thee, that thine all-ness

may be clear to both, and that together we may prostrate ourselves before thy majesty and worship thee as the sovereign Lord of all.

For Zoroaster

215. O GOD, I thank thee for Zoroaster, for his faith in thee as Creator and in man as endowed by thee with free will and immortality. I thank thee for his insight that in individual life and in human history there is a never-ending struggle between good and evil, between truth and falsehood. Arm us in this struggle with the shield of righteousness, the belt of truth, our sword thy word, our feet quick for thy peace, conscious of thy never-failing grace made known to us in Jesus Christ, our Lord.

For India's seekers

216. O GOD OF ALL TRUTH AND GRACE, I thank thee for seekers in India's religious life, for the search for the One behind the many, for the conviction that the spirit of man is akin to thee the universal Spirit, and for the spirit of loving devotion seen in its poets and saints. Lead us from the unreal to the real, from darkness to light and from death to immortality.

Thanksgiving for Jews

217. O GOD, I thank thee for my older brothers and sisters in faith, for their continuing certainty that they are a people of God, for their insights into a divine law by which peoples and nations should live, for their endurance through centuries of persecution and rejection, for their prophets and saints, and for Jesus who lived and died a Jew. Grant that as Christians and Jews come closer together, we may seek thy will for deeper faith in thee and for a service of blessing to humanity, O God of all.

In silence
let us offer grateful hearts to God that he has always been
at work in the spirits of people, inspiring prophets and
saints and willing us into wider truth and deeper
holiness.

54. Praying with Others

Every prayer
> O thou who hearest prayer! To thee shall all flesh come.
>
> *Psalm 65 : 2*

Every voice
> The spirit of the Lord hath filled the world, and that which holdeth all things together hath knowledge of every voice.
>
> *Wisdom 1 : 7*

Every nation
> All the ends of the earth shall remember and turn unto the Lord: and all the kindreds of the nations shall worship before him.
>
> *Psalm 22 : 27*

Everywhere
> Whither shall I go from thy spirit? Or whither shall I flee from thy presence?
>
> *Psalm 139 : 7*

Let us pray

With an Egyptian king

218. CREATOR OF THE GERM IN WOMAN,
      Maker of seed in man,
      Giving life to the son in the body of his mother,
      Soothing him that he may not weep,
      Nurse (even) in the womb,
      Giver of breath to animate every one that he maketh!
      When he cometh forth from the womb . . . on the day
         of his birth,
      Thou openest his mouth in speech,
      Thou suppliest his necessities.
      When the fledgling in the egg chirps in the shell
      Thou givest him breath therein to preserve him
         alive . . .

He goeth about upon his two feet
When he hath come forth therefrom.
How manifold are thy works!
They are hidden from before us
O sole God, whose powers no other possesseth.
Thou didst create the earth according to thy heart.

With the Buddha

219. NOW MAY EVERY LIVING THING, feeble or strong, omitting none, or tall or middle-sized or short, subtle or gross of form, seen or unseen, dwelling near or far away, born or yet unborn, may every living thing be full of bliss.

With Kabir, an Indian poet

220. FROM THE BEGINNING until the end of time there is love between me and thee, and how shall such love be extinguished?

With God's Zoroastrian worshippers

221. MAY OBEDIENCE CONQUER DISOBEDIENCE within this house, and may peace triumph over discord here, and generous giving over avarice, reverence over contempt, speech with truthful words over lying utterance; may the righteous order gain the victory over the demon of the lie.

With God's Sikh children

222. KNOW THAT HE WHO SINGS the praise of God
Thereby practises all religious duties.
He who within a day or night
Contemplates God even for a moment
Loses all fear of death
And illumines his life and self.

With Rabi'ah, a Muslim woman mystic
223. O MY LORD, the stars are shining and the eyes of men
      are closed, and kings have shut their doors and
      every lover is alone with his beloved, and here am I
      alone with thee.

Blessings from African religion
224. MAY GOD GO WITH YOU!
      Go nicely: may your path be swept of danger.
      Let God bear you in peace like a young shoot!
      May you meet with the kindly-disposed one!
      May God take care of you!
      May God walk you well!
      May you pass the night with God!
      May God be with you who remain behind!
      May you stay with God!

Let us in silence
   express our grateful wonder to God for these prayers from
   different faiths and over many centuries.

Let us also pray for the time when people of all faiths
will pray with us
      Our Father who art in heaven, hallowed be thy name,
      thy kingdom come, thy will be done,
      in earth as it is in heaven.
      Give us this day our daily bread
      and forgive us our trespasses
      as we forgive those who trespass against us.
      For thine is the kingdom, the power and the glory
      for ever and ever. *Amen.*

55. True Religion

A prophet's idea of the meaning of religion
He has showed you, O man, what is good; and what does
the Lord require of you but to do justice, and to love
kindness, and to walk humbly with your God.

Micah 6 : 8

A New Testament writer has a similar thought
Religion that is pure and undefiled before God the Father
is this: to visit orphans and widows in their affliction,
and to keep oneself unstained from the world.

James 1 : 27

A good criterion
You will know them by their fruits. Are grapes gathered
from thorns or figs from thistles?

Matthew 7 : 16

In heart and conscience
When Gentiles who have not the law do by nature what
the law requires, they are a law to themselves, even
though they do not have the law. They show that what
the law requires is written on their hearts, which their
conscience also bears witness.

Romans 2 : 14–15

Meditation
People from different organized religions have certain
things in common: all seek to know the origin of the
universe, the meaning of human life, the principles of
the good life, what happens after death, availability of
help from outside oneself, how to explain and deal with
evil, the values by which people should live, the spirituality which people should practise. We ought to be

ready to share what answers others have discovered to these questions, as well as to share with them our own insights.

Let us pray

225. LORD OF ALL POWER AND MIGHT, who art the author and giver of all good things: Graft in our hearts the love of thy name, increase in us true religion, nourish us with all goodness, and of thy great mercy keep us in the same; through Jesus Christ our Lord.

226. ETERNAL LIGHT, shine into our hearts,
eternal goodness, deliver us from evil,
eternal power, be our support,
eternal wisdom, scatter the darkness of our ignorance,
eternal pity, have mercy upon us;
  that with all our heart and mind and soul and strength we may seek thy face and be brought by thine infinite mercy to thy holy presence; through Jesus Christ our Lord.

227. GRANT, O GOD, that we may wait patiently, as servants standing before their lord, to know thy will; that we may welcome all truth, under whatever outward forms it may be uttered; that we may bless every good deed, by whomsoever it may be done; that we may rise above all party strife to the contemplation of the eternal truth and goodness; through Jesus Christ our Saviour.

Down in the heart

Thou hast made us for thyself: our hearts shall find no rest until they find their rest in thee.

56. To the End of Time

The Eternal
> Before the mountains were brought forth, or ever thou hadst formed the earth and the world, from everlasting to everlasting thou art God.
>
> *Psalm 90 : 2*

The divine dimension of time
> For a thousand years in thy sight are but as yesterday when it is past, or as a watch in the night.
>
> *Psalm 90 : 4*

Each generation passes on God's truth
> One generation shall praise thy works to another and shall declare thy mighty acts.
>
> *Psalm 145 : 4*

In difficult times
> Making the most of the time, because the days are evil.
>
> *Ephesians 5 : 15*

When God's purpose is fulfilled
> But of that day or that hour no one knows, not even the angels in heaven, nor the Son, but only the Father.
>
> *Mark 13 : 32*

> Then comes the end when he delivers the kingdom to God the Father after destroying every rule and every authority and power . . . that God may be everything to everyone.
>
> *1 Corinthians 15 : 24, 26*

228. O GOD OF ETERNITY AND CREATOR OF TIME, we know that each generation has to learn afresh of what thou hast done in the past and receive from the passing generation the heritage of faith. Grant that each succeeding generation may take its part in the unfinished task of establishing thy kingdom, keeping alight the torch of faith and receiving from thee grace to prepare for the new order of being which thou hast prepared for us in thy Son, Jesus Christ, our ever-living Lord.

229. ALMIGHTY AND EVERLASTING GOD, who hast set thine eternity in our hearts and awakened within us desires which the world cannot satisfy: lift our eyes, we pray thee, above the narrow horizons of this present world, that we may behold the things eternal in the heaven, wherein is laid up for us an inheritance that fadeth not away; through Jesus Christ our Lord.

230. O LORD, who hast set before us the great hope that thy kingdom shall come, and hast taught us to pray for its coming: give us grace to discern the signs of its dawning, and to work for the perfect day when thy will shall be done on earth as it is in heaven; through Jesus Christ our Lord.

Keep me travelling, O God
with you, here in time, that when I move over the horizon into eternity, I may enjoy you even more fully.

Now unto him who is able to keep us from falling and to present us without blemish before the presence of his glory with rejoicing, to the only God, our Saviour through Jesus Christ our Lord, be glory, majesty, dominion and authority, before all time and now and for ever. *Amen.*

IX. WINNING THE WORLD

57. Fear not, little flock

Fear not, little flock, for it is your Father's good pleasure to
give you the kingdom.

Luke 12 : 32

The seventy returned with joy, saying,
    Lord, even the demons are subject to us in your name!
And he said to them,
    I saw Satan fall like lightning from heaven.
        Behold, I have given you authority to tread upon ser-
    pents and scorpions, and over all the power of the enemy;
    and nothing shall hurt you.
        Nevertheless do not rejoice in this, that the spirits are
    subject to you; but rejoice that your names are written in
    heaven.

Luke 10 : 17–20

For consider your call, brethren; not many of you were wise
    according to worldly standards, not many were powerful,
    not many were of noble birth;
but God chose what is foolish in the world to shame the wise,
    God chose what is weak in the world to shame the strong,
    God chose what is low and despised in the world, even
    things that are not, to bring to nothing things that are, so
    that no human being might boast in the presence of God.

1 Corinthians 1 : 26–29

Let us thank God
>for the sure confidence of his promises
>for our unshakable trust in his calling
>for his never-failing presence within his church

Let us pray
>for the church in lands where Christians are a small
>>minority;
>for the small groups of Christians in countries where
>>Christ may not be openly proclaimed;
>for Christians living in areas of particular difficulty,
>>that they may be brave in their witness and Christ-
>>like in their lives;
>>that we may be faithful in our prayers for them.

231. GRANT UNTO US, O GOD,
>>that we may never be ashamed to confess
>>>the faith of Christ crucified,
>>but may manfully fight under his banner
>>>against sin, the world, and the devil,
>>and continue Christ's faithful soldiers and servants
>>>unto our lives' end.

232. WE BESSECH THEE, O LORD, for all members of thy
holy catholic church throughout the world, that
they may ever remember that, wheresoever there be
a congregation of the faithful, there the Lord of the
church is in the midst.

233. REMEMBER, O LORD, what thou hast wrought in us,
>>and not what we deserve,
>>and as thou has called us to thy service,
>>>make us worthy of our calling;
>>>through Jesus Christ our Lord.

234. O HOLY SPIRIT,
grant us, we pray thee, the gift of courage.
Enable us to live as Jesus lived,
in steadfast opposition to sin
and in courageous faith in the power of God.
As Jesus faced the hatred of enemies
and the desertion of friends on earth,
so may we be prepared to face manfully
and with unfailing faith
whatever opposition or enmity
our service of Christ may arouse against us,
in certain hope that in all things
we can be strengthened through him
who has overcome the world.

235. GOD, who didst allow the swords and staves of
armed men
to oppose the pure majesty of the prince of peace:
Grant us, his disciples,
to fear no threatenings of force
nor assaults of evil,
but to stand immovable in the might of thy Spirit
and the testimony of faith;
through the same Jesus Christ our Lord.

236. WE ADORE THEE, O CHRIST,
and we bless thy holy name
in all thy holy churches that are in all the world,
because by thy holy cross
thou hast redeemed the world. *Amen.*

Two or three
in your name and spirit, dear Lord, are enough for you to
be present in all your love and grace.

58. If the world hate you

Christ's prayer for his followers in times of opposition
I do not pray that thou shouldst take them out of the
world, but that thou shouldst keep them from the evil
one.

John 17 : 15

Christ's followers must expect the treatment that he received
Remember the word that I said to you, A servant is not
greater than his master. If they persecuted me, they will
persecute you; if they kept my word,
they will keep yours also.

John 15 : 20

Opposition brings with it opportunities for witness
I want you to know, brethren, that what has happened to
me has really served to advance the gospel, so that it has
become known throughout the whole praetorian guard
and to all the rest that my imprisonment is for Christ;
and most of the brethren have been made confident in
the Lord because of my imprisonment, and are much
more bold to speak the word of God without fear.

Philippians 1 : 12–14

Let us pray
for our brethren enduring opposition for their faith today,
that they may see opportunities for witness in every
difficulty;
that hope and courage may be strengthened by the knowledge that the whole church is praying for them;
that we ourselves may not shrink from unpopularity,
ridicule and opposition for the sake of our Lord, nor fail
in love towards those who oppose us.

237. LORD JESUS CHRIST, we pray thee for our fellow
Christians in all parts of the world who are facing
difficulties, and who are tempted to turn back
because their way is hard. Make them brave and
steadfast, and may their loyal witness draw others
to thee; for thy name's sake.

Let us pray with a Chinese Christian
238. O LORD, WE PRAY THEE that thy church, in the midst
of tribulations and temptations, may remain steadfast and faithful to thy mission.

May thy followers, in the midst of unpopularity and
persecution, be not ashamed of acknowledging thy
lordship, nor of witnessing to thy gospel of salvation. O God, give them courage, hope and strength
that they may be able to stand the severe tests and
overcome the temptations. May they be conscious
of the fact that Christ is far above all principality
and power and might and dominion, and every
name that is named, not only in this world, but also
in that which is to come.

We pray that through all trials, thy servants may
come out like the Apostle Paul: troubled, yet not
distressed; perplexed, but not in despair; persecuted, but not forsaken; cast down, but not destroyed.

Help them and strengthen them, O Lord. We pray in
the name of Jesus Christ, our Lord and Saviour.

Let the church
bear the sorrow of the world and the wounds inflicted by
the world, and know that it is then your body, dear
Lord.

239. BLESSED ARE YE when men shall reproach you, and
persecute you, and say all manner of evil against
you falsely, for my sake. Rejoice, and be exceeding
glad: for great is your reward in heaven. *Amen.*

161

59. The Church on the Cross

And when they had called in the apostles, they beat them
and charged them not to speak in the name of Jesus, and
let them go.
Then they left the presence of the council, rejoicing that they
were counted worthy to suffer dishonour for the name.
And every day in the temple and at home they did not
cease teaching and preaching Jesus as the Christ.

Acts 5 : 40–42

Beloved, do not be surprised at the fiery ordeal which comes
upon you to prove you, as though something strange were
happening to you. But rejoice in so far as you share
Christ's sufferings, that you may also rejoice and be glad
when his glory is revealed.
If you are reproached for the name of Christ, you are
blessed, because the spirit of glory and of God rests upon
you.

1 Peter 4 : 12–14

We are afflicted in every way, but not crushed; perplexed,
but not driven to despair; persecuted, but not forsaken;
struck down, but not destroyed; always carrying in the
body the death of Jesus, so that the life of Jesus may also
be manifested in our bodies.

2 Corinthians 4 : 8–10

Let us pray
for our brethren in different parts of the world who suffer
for their faith, that they may be more than conquerors
through him who loves them;
for all who are tempted through fear or pain to compromise their faith or deny their Master;
for ourselves that we may never be ashamed to show that
we belong to Christ;
for all who suffer for making a stand for truth and right.

240. ALMIGHTY GOD, who hast shown us in the life and
teaching of thy Son the true way of blessedness,
thou hast also shown us in his suffering and death
that the path of love may lead to the cross, and the
reward of faithfulness may be a crown of thorns.
Give us grace to learn these hard lessons.
May we take up our cross and follow Christ, in the
strength of patience and the constancy of faith; and
see even in our darkest hour of trial and anguish the
shining of the eternal light.

241. O ALMIGHTY GOD, who hast taught us that they who
suffer for thee shall see of the travail of their souls
and shall be satisfied, and that they who pour out
their souls unto death shall divide the spoil with the
strong:
We thank thee that in the cross of thy dear Son thou
hast revealed the secret of spiritual victory out of
utter defeat, and that the obedience of Good Friday
shall lead to the triumph of Easter.
Keep this faith before the eyes of our brethren who
suffer for thee, and transform our prayers into courage and love for them.

242. O LORD CHRIST, who, when thine hour was come,
didst go without fear among those who sought thy
life: Grant us grace to confess thee before men,
without arrogance and without fear, that thy holy
name may be glorified.

While any evil remains
it is certain to oppose any goodness, or at last give in to the
perfection of your love, dear God.

243.   BE IN ALL WHO SUFFER FOR THEE, O CHRIST,
       and give them thy steadfast strength,
         that as they suffer for thee,
         thou mayest be in them
       and carry them and their cross to victory and life.

60. Interceding

Our Lord's command and promise
Ask, and it will be given you; seek and you will find;
knock, and it will be opened to you.
For every one who asks receives, and he who seeks finds,
and to him who knocks it will be opened.

Matthew 7 : 7–8

If you abide in me, and my words abide in you, ask
whatever you will, and it shall be done for you.

John 15 : 7

Prayer for the church's mission
When he saw the crowds, he had compassion for them,
because they were harassed and helpless, like sheep without a shepherd. Then he said to his disciples,
The harvest is plentiful, but the labourers are few;
pray therefore the Lord of the harvest to send out
labourers into his harvest.

Matthew 9 : 36–38

A missionary's request for prayer
Continue steadfastly in prayer, being watchful in it with
thanksgiving; and pray for us also, that God may open
to us a door for the word, to declare the mystery of
Christ, on account of which I am in prison, that I may
make it clear, as I ought to speak.

Colossians 4 : 2–4

Meditation
The best prayer of all is that God's will shall be done in
and for those for whom we pray.
Prayer assumes that we are trying to co-operate with
God's will.

    to wait often upon you, in silence and stillness, wanting
       nothing but your good and loving will for myself, the
       church and the world.

244.   Lord, help me to pray,
            to desire to pray,
            to delight to pray.
    Make all my supplication joyful with faith,
          joyful with hope,
          joyful with love:
Joyful with thine own Spirit interceding with me,
    urgent with his yearning behind my inattention,
    wide with his wisdom behind my dim-sightedness,
    burning with his fire behind my lukewarmth:
Joyful in the fellowship of the prayers of thy saints,
         and of thy whole church, above, below;
through him who in heaven maketh intercession
           continually,
        thy Son Jesus Christ our Lord.

Let us also pray with Paul
245.   O Father of our Lord Jesus Christ,
    from whom every family in heaven and on earth is
       named:
    Grant that, according to the riches of thy glory,
we may be strengthened with power through thy Spirit,
    that Christ may dwell in our hearts by faith;
    that we, being rooted and grounded in love,
    may be strong to apprehend with all the saints
what is the length and breadth and height and depth,
and to know the love of Christ which passeth knowledge.

246. WE PRAY THEE, O LORD OUR FATHER, for all who profess and call themselves Christians, that their love may abound yet more and more unto the day of Christ; that they may be sincere and void of offence, being filled with the fruits of righteousness which are through Jesus Christ unto thy praise and glory, now and for ever.

247. GOD FORBID that I should sin against the Lord in ceasing to pray for you. *Amen.*

61. More blessed to give

We want you to know, brethren, about the grace of God
   which has been shown in the churches of Macedonia,
for in a severe test of affliction, their abundance of joy and
   their extreme poverty have overflowed in a wealth of liber-
   ality on their part. For they gave according to their means,
   as I can testify, and beyond their means, of their own free
   will . . .
   but first they gave themselves to the Lord.

2 Corinthians 8 : 1–3, 5

He looked up and saw the rich putting their gifts into the
   treasury; and he saw a poor widow put in two copper
   coins. And he said,
      Truly I tell you, this poor widow has put in more than
      all of them; for they all contributed out of their abun-
      dance, but she out of her poverty put in all the living
      that she had.

Luke 21 : 1–4

In all things I have shown you that by so toiling one must
help the weak, remembering the words of the Lord Jesus,
how he said,
      It is more blessed to give than to receive.

Acts 20 : 35 (A.V.)

Let us remember
      that the church depends on the gifts of its faithful people to
      carry on its mission to the world
      that we do not give much to God if we only provide
      amenities for our own local church
      that our Lord accepts all we do to relieve the needs of
      others as if it were done to himself
      that our money and possessions are to be held in a spirit of
      stewardship.

248. O GOD, WHO DESIREST no sacrifice,
      but a humble and contrite spirit;
   who wilt accept no gifts,
      save such as come from a good and honest heart:
   Save us, we pray thee, lest we come before thee
      with hands not free from stain;
   and mercifully accept the offering of ourselves,
      who have nothing worthy to offer
         but what is from thee,
      and dare not offer
      what is not hallowed by thee;
         for Jesus Christ's sake.

249. O ALMIGHTY GOD, whose blessed Son
            though he was rich
            yet for our sakes did become poor,
         that we through his poverty might become rich:
   Grant us the spirit of generous self-giving
      that we may further the work of thy church
         and relieve those who are in need.
   Help us who have received so freely from thee
         to give as freely in our turn,
      and so share the blessedness of giving
      as well as the happiness of receiving.
   We ask this in the name of him who gave himself
      for the life of the world,
         even thy Son, Jesus Christ, our Lord.

250. THINE, O LORD, is the greatness, and the power,
      and the glory, and the victory, and the majesty:
   for all that is in the heaven and in the earth is mine;
      thine is the kingdom, O Lord,
      and thou art exalted as head above all.
         All things come of thee,
      and of thine own have we given thee. *Amen.*

If it is true, Lord
   that giving is more blessed than receiving, then it must
   indeed be blessed.

62. Who will go for us?

Then flew one of the seraphim to me, having in his hand a
burning coal which he had taken with tongs from the altar.
And he touched my mouth, and said:
Behold, this has touched your lips; your guilt is taken
away, and your sin forgiven.
And I heard the voice of the Lord saying,
Whom shall I send, and who will go for us?
Then I said, Here I am! Send me.

Isaiah 6 : 6–8

But how are men to call upon him in whom they have not
believed? And how are they to believe in him of whom
they have never heard? And how are they to hear without
a preacher? And how can men preach unless they are sent?
As it is written, How beautiful are the feet of those who
preach good news!

Romans 10 : 14, 15

All authority in heaven and on earth has been given to me.
Go therefore and make disciples of all nations, baptizing
them in the name of the Father and of the Son and of the
Holy Spirit, teaching them to observe all that I have commanded you;
and lo, I am with you always, to the close of the age.

Matthew 28 : 18–20

Let us pray
that Christians everywhere may realize that there is no
participation in Christ without participation in his mission to the world;
that the church may be conscious of its calling as the body
of Christ to fulfil this mission;
for the missionary societies which for many generations
have accepted the responsibility for this work, often
when the church's sense of mission has been weak;

for mission boards and councils through which the
churches now seek to fulfil their obligation;
that Christians everywhere may offer themselves willingly
in this service.

Let my soul reply, O God
with Mary of Nazareth, 'Be it unto me according to your
word.'

251.   O GOD OUR FATHER, help us to realize the greatness of
our calling in Christ. Fill us with fresh visions of thy
love, thy power, thy wonderful purpose for thy
creation; inspire and strengthen us with the sense of
being called in the body of Christ—made one with
our Lord, and in him with one another.

252.   O LORD, without whom our labour is but lost,
and with whom thy little ones go forth as the mighty:
Be present to all works in thy church
which are undertaken according to thy will;
and grant to thy labourers a pure intention,
patient faith, sufficient success upon earth,
and the bliss of serving thee in heaven;
through Jesus Christ our Lord.

253.   GRANT, WE PRAY THEE, O LORD, to all who serve thee
in the organization of the world mission of thy
church the vision of thy purpose for the world, a
share of thy love for men, and a faith that will not
be daunted by difficulty or lack of response.
Let them ever be mindful that thy kingdom is
advanced not by might nor by power, but by thy
Spirit.
Help them to believe that if they first seek thy kingdom and thy righteousness they shall receive sufficient grace for the doing of thy will.
We ask this in the name of Jesus Christ, our Lord.

63. Spreading the Truth

Every man needs the Christian message in his own language
> We hear them telling in their own tongues the mighty
> works of God. *Acts 2 : 11*

The word can be passed on from one church to another
> And when this letter has been read among you, have it
> read also in the church of the Laodiceans, and see that
> you read also the letter from Laodicea. *Colossians 4 : 16*

Three-fifths of the people in the world cannot yet read
> Have you not read this scripture? . . . *Mark 12 : 10*

> Have ye not read what was said to you by God? . . .
> *Matthew 22 : 31*

New methods of communication can help to spread the gospel
> Their voice goes out through all the earth, and their words
> to the end of the world. *Psalm 19 : 4*

> He sends forth his command to the earth; his word runs
> swiftly. *Psalm 147 : 15*

Let us meditate on the power of the printed word—
> it can bring the thought of the writer to many readers;
> it can be produced in thousands of copies;
> it can link the centuries and refresh the memory;
> it can be hidden and read in secret;
> it can remain behind when people have to leave.
> But it is of no value unless people are able to read.

—and on the modern methods of communication
> which can bring news so quickly from one part of the
> world to another;
> which can speak to people in their own homes;
> which can be used to spread lies, suspicion and hatred, or
> truth, trust, and understanding friendship;
> which can enable pictures of happenings and conditions of
> life in one country to be seen by people in many others.

Let us pray
    for writers and artists,
        translators and journalists,
        printers and booksellers,
        teachers of the illiterate,
        broadcasters in television and radio,
    that through them the knowledge of truth, beauty, love
      and goodness may be spread throughout the world;
    for all engaged in spreading the gospel of Christ, that they
      may use every available means;
    for all who cannot yet read, that their fellow men will help
      them to do so and enable them to find truth and that
      new life which is God's will for them.

What a wonderful universe
    we live in, O Creator God. May it also be united in a
    commonwealth, where all may live in peace, free from
    fear, want and injustice.

254. DIRECT AND BLESS, WE BESEECH THEE, LORD, those who
      in this our generation speak where many listen, and
      write what many read, and televise what many see;
      that they may do their part in making the heart of the
      people wise, its mind sound, and its will righteous; to
      the honour of Jesus Christ our Lord.

255. O ALMIGHTY GOD, WE THANK THEE
      for the wonderful universe thou hast created
      and for its secrets revealed to men.
    We thank thee that men may speak to one another
      across the centuries and across the continents,
      annihilating space and time.
    Grant that all means of communication may be used
      for the purpose of truth, peace and love,
      so that all men may hear the good news of the
      gospel and find their brotherhood in thee,
    through Jesus Christ, thine own eternal Word.

256.   BLESSING, and glory, and wisdom, and thanksgiving,
        and honour, and power, and might,
        be unto our God for ever and ever. *Amen.*

X. LAST THINGS

64. The Lord from Heaven

Since all things are thus to be dissolved,
    what sort of persons ought you to be
    in lives of holiness and godliness,
    waiting for and hastening the coming
        of the day of God? . . .
But according to his promise we wait for new heavens and a
    new earth in which righteousness dwells.

2 Peter 3 : 11–13

Then comes the end,
    when he delivers the kingdom to God the Father
        after destroying every rule
        and every authority and power.
For he must reign
    until he has put all his enemies under his feet.
    The last enemy to be destroyed is death . . .
When all things are subjected to him,
    then the Son himself will also be subjected
    to him who put all things under him,
    that God may be everything to every one.

1 Corinthians 15 : 24–26, 28

And this gospel of the kingdom will be preached
    throughout the whole world,
    as a testimony to all nations;
        and then the end will come.

Matthew 24 : 14

Let us remember
>that one day our Lord will return in majesty and judgement;
>
>that only the Father knows the time of the end;
>
>that we are living in the last days, the age between our Lord's first and second comings.

Let us pray
>that we may so live that when our Lord comes he may find us faithful, watchful, expectant;
>
>that by preaching the gospel to all nations we may hasten the time of his coming;
>
>that as we came from God, we may go to God and ever belong to God.

257.   MAKE US, WE BESEECH THEE, O LORD,
>watchful and heedful in awaiting the coming
>of thy Son Christ our Lord;
>that when he shall stand at the door and knock,
>he may find us
>not sleeping in carelessness and sin,
>but awake and rejoicing in his praises;
>through the same Jesus Christ our Lord.

258.   WITHHOLD NOT FROM ME, O MY GOD,
>the best, the Spirit of thy dear Son:
>that in that day when the judgement is set
>I may be presented unto thee
>not blameless, but forgiven,
>not effectual, but faithful,
>not holy, but persevering,
>without desert, but accepted,
>because he hath pleaded the causes of my soul,
>and redeemed my life.

259.   O SAVIOUR CHRIST, we pray thee
>for the millions who have never heard thy name or
>known thy love.

Make thyself known to them
in whatever state they be,
in this world or the next.
Help us to proclaim thy gospel
in urgency and love,
that men may not be left
to live without thee
or die without thee,
but may know with us the joy
of sin forgiven,
of overflowing grace,
of peace in life and death,
and of good things prepared
for them that love thee.
O Saviour of the world, fetch them home
that they may be saved for ever.

Let me always
judge myself by you, dear Lord, so I shall be safe at any
moment of divine judgement.

260. THE GOD OF PEACE himself sanctify you wholly;
and may your spirit and soul and body
be preserved entire,
without blame
at the coming of our Lord Jesus Christ. *Amen.*

65. Where Judgement Begins

Our Lord's presence always brings judgement

Behold, I send my messenger to prepare the way before me, and the Lord whom you seek will suddenly come to his temple; the messenger of the covenant in whom you delight, behold, he is coming, says the Lord of hosts.

But who can endure the day of his coming, and who can stand when he appears?

For he is like a refiner's fire and like fullers' soap; he will sit as a refiner and purifier of silver, and he will purify the sons of Levi and refine them like gold and silver, till they present right offerings to the Lord.   *Malachi 3 : 1–3*

A warning

But if some of the branches were broken off, and you, a wild olive shoot, were grafted in their place to share the richness of the olive tree, do not boast over the branches. If you do boast, remember it is not you that support the root, but the root that supports you.

Romans 11 : 17–21

The need for repentance

But I have this against you, that you have abandoned the love you had at first.

Remember then from what you have fallen, repent and do the works you did at first. If not, I will come to you and remove your lampstand from its place, unless you repent ...

He who has an ear, let him hear what the Spirit says to the churches.

To him who conquers I will grant to eat of the tree of life, which is in the paradise of God.   *Revelation 2 : 4, 5, 7*

O Lord, forgive

our failure to see in Jesus Christ the Lord of all good life, and the Saviour of all mankind.

O Lord, forgive

our coldness and lack of zeal for the kingdom of God,

our past unfaithfulness to Christ's commission to his church,

our tendency to put loyalty to our country before loyalty to the kingdom of God,

our temptations to compromise with the world and to acquiesce in situations which we know to be wrong,

our frequent failures to champion social justice and to be the hope of depressed and suffering peoples,

our failure to lay to heart the divisions of Christ's body,

our small sacrifices, our neglected opportunities, our forgetfulness of those who need the support of our prayers.

O Lord, forgive.

261. O LORD, WE BESEECH THEE, let thy continual pity cleanse and defend thy church; and, because it cannot continue in safety without thy succour, preserve it evermore by thy help and goodness; through Jesus Christ our Lord.

262. O MOST MERCIFUL FATHER,
we confess that we have done little
to forward thy kingdom in the world,
and to advance thy glory.
We would humble ourselves before thee
for our past neglects,
and seek for thy forgiveness.
Pardon our shortcomings.
Give us greater zeal for thy glory.
Make us more ready and more diligent
by our prayers, by our alms,
and by our lives,
to spread abroad the knowledge of thy truth,
and to enlarge the boundaries of thy kingdom.
May the love of Christ constrain us,
and the power of the Holy Spirit renew us,
that we may serve thee more worthily
in the days to come;
through Jesus Christ our Lord.

You are right, O Lord
to be severe on the church, for you have given it a pattern
for its life and the grace needed to live by your stan-
dards.

263.   THE GOD OF PATIENCE and of comfort
grant you to be of the same mind
one with another
according to Christ Jesus:
that with one accord
ye may with one mouth glorify
the God and Father of our Lord Jesus Christ.

Amen.

66. Sir, we would see Jesus

Now there were certain Greeks among those that went up to
    worship at the feast; these therefore came to Philip, which
    was of Bethsaida of Galilee, and asked him, saying,
Sir, we would see Jesus.

John 12 : 20–21 (R.V.)

Now when they saw the boldness of Peter and John, and
    perceived that they were uneducated, common men, they
    wondered; and they recognized that they had been with
    Jesus.

Acts 4 : 13

Have this mind among yourselves, which you have in Christ
    Jesus,
who, though he was in the form of God, did not count
    equality with God a thing to be grasped, but emptied
    himself, taking the form of a servant, being born in the
    likeness of men.
And being found in human form he humbled himself and
    became obedient unto death, even death on a cross.

Philippians 2 : 5–8

Let us reflect
    on the world's demand that is shall see Jesus
        in the life of his church
        and in the lives of individual Christians.
    From every part of the world comes abundant testimony
        that the more Christians have conformed to the spirit of
        Christ the more have people been drawn to Christ and
        his church.
    It is in the lives of ordinary Christians,
        more even than in the gospel pages
        or in the official teaching of the church,
    that non-Christians will judge Christianity
        and our Lord himself.

the world's demand that your followers should be like
their Master. Help me to have your mind and day by
day to grow more like you.

264. O Christ, whose wondrous birth meaneth nothing
        unless we be born again,
      whose death and sacrifice nothing
        unless we die unto sin,
      whose resurrection nothing if thou be risen alone:
      Raise and exalt us, O Saviour,
        both now to the estate of grace
        and hereafter to the state of glory;
      where with the Father and the Holy Spirit
        thou livest and reignest,
            God for ever and ever.

265. O God, the God of all goodness and of all grace,
        who art worthy of a greater love
        than we can either give or understand:
      Fill our hearts, we beseech thee,
          with such love toward thee
          that nothing may seem too hard for us to do
              or to suffer
          in obedience to thy will;
      and grant that thus loving thee,
        we may become daily more like unto thee,
      and finally obtain the crown of life
      which thou hast promised to those that love thee;
        through Jesus Christ our Lord.

Prayer of a Chinese woman after learning to read
266. We are going home to many who cannot read.
        So, Lord, make us to be Bibles
      so that those who cannot read the Book
          can read it in us.

267. Whatsoever we do, in word or in deed,
        may we do all in the name of the Lord Jesus,
        giving thanks to God the Father through him.

67. The Last Trumpet

A warning note
> We shall not all sleep, but we shall all be changed, in a moment, in the twinkling of an eye, at the last trumpet.
>
> *1 Corinthians 15 : 51–52*

A necessary change
> For this perishable nature must put on the imperishable, and this mortal nature must put on immortality.
>
> *1 Corinthians 15 : 53*

Something far better
> My desire is to depart and be with Christ, for that is far better.
>
> *Philippians 1 : 23*

Still in his hands
> Father, into thy hands I commit my spirit.
>
> *Luke 23 : 46*

Fear is the enemy
> And deliver all those who through fear of death were subject to lifelong bondage.
>
> *Hebrews 2 : 15*

Let us reflect
> Death comes to everyone; the certainty of it is like a warning trumpet; death is part of God's ordering of human life, and so it must be part of his loving purpose.
> In the faith of the New Testament, death is as easy and natural as falling asleep here and waking up there; death is our final birth into the spiritual and the eternal; often when death comes it is peaceful, as if someone were whispering 'It is I, don't be afraid.'

Prayers
268. O GOD, we thy creatures try to evade the fact of death, and to keep it out of mind, yet in our deeper

moments we know it is a warning note, urging us so to die every day to all selfishness and sin, that when the time comes for our final migration, we may take death in our stride because life is so strong within us, as it was in him who was so manifestly thy true Son and so convincingly the prototype of thy finished humanity, even Jesus Christ, thy Son, our brother.

269. WE GIVE BACK TO YOU, O GOD, those whom you gave to us. You did not lose them when you gave them to us, and we do not lose them by their return to you. Your dear Son has taught us that life is eternal and love cannot die. So death is only a horizon, and a horizon is only the limit of our sight. Open our eyes to see more clearly, and draw us closer to you, that we may know that we are nearer to our loved ones who are with you. You have told us that you are preparing a place for us: prepare us also for that happy place, that where you are we may also be always, O dear Lord of life and death.

270. O GOD, the heart fails in the thought of the millions who die before they find the full enjoyment of life as you intend it to be—deaths through war, hunger, violence and disease. We know that you are the giver and sustainer of life, extending it beyond man's short span, into the spiritual and eternal. O God, I dare to ask for eternal life for every soul, now and beyond death: I pray this prayer through my touch with Jesus Christ, eternal Son and eternal brother.

We need not fear death
for it is the gateway to more life
the going to the Father of all souls
our final birth into the spiritual
and the eternal.

68. According to your Faith

According to your faith be it done to you.

If you have faith as a grain of mustard seed, you will say to
this mountain, Move hence to yonder place, and it will
move; and nothing will be impossible to you.

Matthew 9 : 29; 17 : 20

With men it is impossible, but not with God;
for all things are possible with God.
All things are possible to him who believes.

Mark 10 : 27; 9 : 23

This is the victory that overcomes the world, our faith.

1 John 5 : 4

Now faith is the assurance of things hoped for, the conviction
of things not seen . . .
For Moses endured as seeing him who is invisible.

Hebrews 11 : 1, 27

For I know whom I have believed. *2 Timothy 1 : 12*

Let us pray
271. LORD, WE BELIEVE IN THEE, help thou our unbelief;
we love thee, yet not with perfect hearts as we would;
we long for thee, yet not with our full strength;
we trust in thee, yet not with our whole mind.
Accept our faith, our love,
our longing to know and serve thee,
our trust in thy power to keep us.
What is cold do thou kindle,
what is lacking do thou supply;
through Jesus Christ our Lord.

272. O LORD OUR GOD, in whose hands is the issue of all things, who requirest from thy stewards not success, but faithfulness:

Give us such faith in thee, and in thy sure purpose, that we measure not our lives by what we have done, or failed to do, but by our obedience to thy will.

273. O THOU WHO ART HEROIC LOVE, keep alive in our hearts that adventurous spirit which makes men scorn the way of safety, so that thy will be done.

For so only shall we worthy of those courageous souls who in every age have ventured all in obedience to thy call, and for whom the trumpets have sounded on the other side; through Jesus Christ our Lord.

O Lord, I know
that faith is most faith in moments of doubt, trembling or temptation. Lord, increase my faith.

274. LORD, INCREASE MY FAITH,
that I may embrace everything that is thy will.
Lord, increase my faith,
that the mountains of difficulty may be removed.
Lord, increase my faith that I may never be
at loss for some creative action for thee.
Lord, increase my faith that I may never be
impatient or frustrated.
Lord, increase my faith that I may run to thee
in every situation.
Lord, increase my faith that I may trust thee
in seeming failure or defeat.
Lord, increase my faith that I may endure
as seeing thee who art visible only to the eye of
faith.
Lord, fill me with faith, hope and love,
this day and always.

69. Jesus Only

After this many of his disciples drew back and no longer
went about with him.
Jesus said to the twelve, Will you also go away?
Simon Peter answered him, Lord, to whom shall we go?
You have the words of eternal life; and we have believed,
and have come to know, that you are the Holy One of
God.

John 6 : 66–69

But whatever gain I had, I counted as loss for the sake of
Christ. Indeed I count everything as loss because of the
surpassing worth of knowing Christ Jesus my Lord.
For his sake I have suffered the loss of all things, and count
them as refuse, in order that I may gain Christ . . . that I
may know him and the power of his resurrection, and may
share his sufferings, becoming like him in his death.

Philippians 3 : 7, 8, 10

I have been crucified with Christ; it is no longer I who live,
but Christ who lives in me; and the life I now live in the
flesh I live by faith in the Son of God, who loved me and
gave himself for me.

Galatians 2 : 20

I know whom I have believed, and I am persuaded that he is
able to guard that which I have committed unto him
against that day.

2 Timothy 1 : 12 (R.V.)

Jesus Christ is the same yesterday and today and for ever.

Hebrews 13 : 8

Let us remember
the faith of the evangelists that with the death of Christ the
curtain between man and God was torn from the top to
the bottom

the faith that in Christ all walls of partition are broken
down

the promise of our Lord that he is with us to the end of the
world

that every soul can be a temple of his presence

that his grace is sufficient for every difficulty, every temptation, every opportunity and every adventure.

Christ's uniqueness

275. O GOD, there has never been anyone quite like Jesus,
who knows you so intimately, who is so open to
your inspiration, who loves people as you do, who
shares your plans, yet knows us humans because he
is one of us. O God, I thank you for him, I come to
you through him, I will try to grow like him, I will
enlist under him to work for the world you want,
and to bring your love and blessing into every single
life, O God and Father of Jesus Christ.

Christ Within

276. O CHRIST MY LORD, I pray that you will turn my
heart to you in the depths of being, where with the
noise of creatures silenced and the clamour of both-
ersome thoughts stilled, I shall stay with you, where
I find you always present and where I love and
worship you.

Christ on every road

277. O Christ, my way
to the God of all salvation,
men of other faiths
believe they have their own salvation faith.
Be with them, dear Lord,
to encourage them on their way
to their own Jerusalem
so that we all find ourselves
with the spirits of just men made perfect
in the presence of the eternal God,
the God of many names,
Creator, Lover, Saviour of us all.

Dedication

278. O Lord Jesus Christ, who hast created and redeemed me, and hast brought me unto that which now I am, thou knowest what thou wouldst do with me; do with me according to thy will; for thy tender mercy's sake.

I accept, O Lord

the world's demand that I should be like the one I profess and dare to preach. Fulfil your promise that one day this disciple shall be as his Master.

70. Come and Worship

God is spirit, and those who worship him must worship in
spirit and truth . . .
for such the Father seeks to worship him.   *John 4 : 24, 23*

Worship the Lord in holy array; tremble before him, all the
earth! Say among the nations,
The Lord reigns! Yea, the world is established, it shall
never be moved; he will judge the peoples with equity.

Psalm 96 : 9, 10

Great and wonderful are thy deeds, O Lord God the
Almighty!
Just and true are thy ways, O king of the ages!
Who shall not fear and glorify thy name, O Lord?
For thou alone art holy.
All nations shall come and worship thee,
for thy judgements have been revealed.   *Revelation 15 : 3, 4*

Let us remember
the saints, martyrs and angels before God's throne,
unceasing in their worship
before the unclouded vision of God;
the church throughout the world,
never silent in the worship of God;
the primary duty of men—to worship God the Creator;
that worship is the most effective cure for self-centredness.

Let us pray
for a deepening sense of worship as we behold the unfold-
ing wonder of the universe;
for hearts full of praise as we understand more clearly
God's great purpose of love for the world;
for Christians of all nations, that in the common faith they
may express their worship in differing ways, native to
their own heritage;

that as churches come together in unity, their worship
   may be deepened and enriched by the contribution
   which each one brings;
that as the great religions converge we may share with one
   another the treasures of spirituality.

279. O my God,
      if I worship thee in desire for heaven,
         exclude me from heaven;
      If I worship thee for fear of hell,
         burn me in hell.
      But if I worship thee for thyself alone,
         then withhold not from me thine eternal beauty.

280. Almighty God, unto whom all hearts be open, all
      desires known, and from whom no secrets are hid:
      Cleanse the thoughts of our hearts by the inspiration
         of thy Holy Spirit, that we may perfectly love thee,
         and worthily magnify thy holy name;
      through Christ our Lord.

281. Grant to me, O Lord, to worship thee
            in spirit and in truth;
            to submit all my nature to thee,
      that my conscience may be quickened by thy holiness,
            my mind nourished by thy truth,
            my imagination purified by thy beauty.
      Help me to open my heart to thy love
      and to surrender my will to thy purpose.
            So may I lift up my heart to thee
            in selfless adoration and love.
            Through Jesus Christ my Lord.

When I truly worship
    I forget myself, O God, and know the hope and promise of
    salvation in the consciousness of your love, your all-ness
    and your eternity.

282.   O Praise God in his holiness;
       praise him according to his excellent greatness . . .
      Let everything that hath breath praise the Lord.

COMMITMENT TO JESUS CHRIST

283.   JESUS CHRIST, I want you:
        for my own sake,
        for your sake,
        for the sake of others.

      I want you for my own sake:
        because I am nothing,
        because I am so weak,
        because I am a sinner.

      I want you for your sake:
        that I may know you,
        that I may love you,
        that I may become like you.

      I want you for the sake of others:
        that I may do them no harm,
        that I may do them only good,
        that I may give you to them.

   JESUS CHRIST, you want me:
        for my sake,
        for your own sake,
        for the sake of others.

      You want me for my sake:
        because you made me,
        because you died for me,
        because you have chosen me.

You want me for your own sake:
    that your joy may be in me,
    that where you are I also may be,
    that you may live in me.

You want me for the sake of others:
    that through me you may heal them,
    that through me you may teach them,
    that through me you may live in them.

THEN, JESUS CHRIST,
    take as your right,
    receive as my gift,
    all my liberty, my memory,
        my understanding, my will
        all that I have,
        all that I am,
        all that I can be.
Thou hast given it all to me:
    to thee, O Lord, I restore it.
All is thine:
    dispose of it according to thy will.

Give me thy love,
give me thy grace,
    and I am rich enough.
Nor ask I anything beside.

A NOTE ON SOURCES

1. Revelation 4 : 11 R.V.
2. Hebrews 1 : 10–12 R.V.
3. Wisdom 11 : 24–26
4. Liturgy of St. James. *Prayers New and Old*, A. W. Robinson (Student Christian Movement Press)
5. *Daily Prayer*, Compiled by Eric Milner-White & G. W. Briggs (Oxford University Press)
6. Nestorian Liturgy, *Daily Prayer*
7. Luke 1 : 68–69
8. *Book of Common Prayer* (B.C.P.)
9. *New Every Morning* (British Broadcasting Corporation)
10. *Daily Prayer*
11. *A Devotional Diary*, arr. J. H. Oldham (S.C.M. Press)
12. Based on *Brihadaranyaka Upanishad* I : 3, 27, before 600 B.C.
13. *B.C.P.* as proposed 1928
14. Eric Fenn. *New Every Morning*
15. *After the Third Collect*, ed. E. Milner-White (Mowbray)
16. *Per Christum Vinces*, Compiled by E. M. Barton (Longmans, Green)
17. *Daily Prayer*
18. George Appleton (G.A.)
19. Romans 15 : 13 R.V.
20. *Prayers of the World-Wide Church*, (Society for the Propagation of the Gospel)
21. Te Deum Laudamus
22. Eric Fenn. *New Every Morning*
23. G.A.
24. G.A.
25. Bishop Andrewes
26. G.A.
27. Psalm 145 : 10–13
28. *Christian News-Letter*
29. Revelation 5 : 13 R.S.V.
30. *Prayers of the World-Wide Church*
31. C.M.J. (adapted)
32. *B.C.P.*
33. G.A.
34. Psalm 72 : 18, 19
35. *After the Third Collect*
36. *Prayers New and Old*
37. *The Church in Germany in Prayer*, trs. Walter Kagerah and Robert A. S. Martineau (Mowbray)
38. *B.C.P.*
39. *See* Revelation 14
40. *A War Primer* (S.P.C.K.)
41. By a Christian of the Hervey Islands, in *The World at One in Prayer*, ed. Daniel Johnson Fleming (Harper Bros.)
42. *Christian News-Letter*
43. *The Life that is Light*, Archbishop Goodier, adapted (Burns Oates & Washbourne)
44. Freely adapted from Jeremy Taylor. *Daily Prayer*

45. *Meditations and Prayers*, Evelyn Underhill (Longmans, Green)
46. Archbishop William Temple
47. *With Christ in God*, S. C. Hughson (S.P.C.K. and Holy Cross Press, New York)
48. *B.C.P.*
49. *A War Primer*
50. By a Nigerian Christian, in *World Dominion XII* (1934), (World Dominion Press)
51. Mozarabic, trs. W. Bright. *Daily Prayer*
52. Erasmus
53. Christian Prayers, 1578. *Daily Prayer*
54. By an African Christian teacher, in *The World at One in Prayer*
55. *A War Primer*
56. Collect for Easter Day, *B.C.P.*
57. Eric Fenn. *New Every Morning*
58. Source untraced
59. Bishop Cotton
60. G.A.
61. Bishop Palmer. *Prayers of the World-Wide Church*
62. G.A.
63. Methodist Covenant Service. *The Book of Offices* (Epworth Press)
64. St. Augustine (354–430)
65. *B.C.P.*
66. Bishop Westcott
67. Dr. E. B. Pusey, (1800–1882)
68. Jeremy Taylor, *Jubilee of a Penitent Soul*
69. *B.C.P.*
70. Dean Vaughan. *Daily Prayer*
71. Jeremy Taylor, adapted. *After the Third Collect*
72. Dean Vaughan. *Daily Prayer*
73. *My God My Glory*, E. Milner-White (S.P.C.K.)
74. *New Every Morning*
75. St. Gregory, (540–604)
76. *New Every Morning*
77. Hebrews 13 : 20–21 A.V.
78. G.A.
79. *B.C.P.*
80. Mozarabic Liturgy
81. G.A.
82. Revelation 5 : 13 R.V.
83. *The Book of Common Order* (of the Church of Scotland) O.U.P.
84. *B.C.P.*
85. G.A.
86. Tenth Century
87. *A Procession of Passion Prayers*, E. Milner-White (S.P.C.K.)
88. Liturgy of St. Mark
89. *Daily Prayer*
90. *The Book of Common Order* (of the Church of Scotland)
91. *The Life that is Light* (adapted)
92. G.A.
93. *The Life that is Light* (adapted)
94. Psalm 103 : 1–4
95. Luke 1 : 68, 77–79
96. *B.C.P.* 1928
97. *Prayers of the World-Wide Church*
98. *Ancient Collects*, trs. W. Bright
99. U.S.P.G. (adapted)
100. 2 Corinthians 1 : 3–4
101. *A Book of Prayers for Schools* (S.C.M. Press) adapted
102. *Prayers of the World-Wide Church*
103. Thomas à Kempis (adapted)
104. *The Kingdom, the Power and the Glory*
105. *The Kingdom, the Power and the Glory*
106. *A Book of Prayers for Schools*
107. *See* Psalm 104 : 14, 15
108. Bishop Paget. *Daily Prayer*
109. G.A.
110. St. Francis of Assisi. *Daily Prayer*
111. Hebrews 13 : 20–21 A.V.
112. *A Pocketful of Prayers* (Toc H)
113. *Prayers of Citizenship*, K. T. Henderson (Longmans, Green)
114. *Prayers for use in an Indian College*, J. S. Hoyland (S.P.C.K.)
115. J. H. Jowett (adapted). *A*

Chain of Prayer Across the Ages (Murray)
116. Reinhold Niebuhr
117. Bishop John Taylor
118. Ephesians 3 : 20–21
119. G.A.
120. B.C.P.
121. George Adam Smith
122. G.A.
123. Romans 15 : 13 R.V.
124. *Daily Prayer*
125. B.C.P.
126. *New Every Morning*
127. *Daily Prayer*
128. B.C.P.
129. *Daily Prayer*
130. Muhammad d. A.D. 632
131. Based on Ephesians 3 : 17–19
132. *After the Third Collect*
133. Dean Vaughan. *Daily Prayer*
134. *Prayers for Common Use* (U.M.C.A.)
135. *See* Psalm 67
136. *Jerusalem Chamber Fellowship of Prayer*
137. *A Procession of Passion Prayers*
138. Roman Missal. *Daily Prayer*
139. G.A.
140. Olive Wyon
141. *New Every Morning*
142. *My God My Glory*
143. Romans 16 : 25–27
144. *New Every Morning*
145. B.C.P.
146. *Daily Prayer*
147. Liturgy of St. Mark, trs. W. Bright (adapted)
148. G.A.
149. Gothic Missal, A.D. 1680
150. *Acts of Devotion* (S.P.C.K.)
151. *Prayers in Use at Uppingham School*, R. H. Owen (O.U.P.)
152. I Peter 5 : 10–11 A.V.
153. *A Book of Prayers for Schools*
154. Collect for All Saints' Day, B.C.P.
155. G.A.
156. Revelation 15 : 3
157. B.C.P.

158. *Prayers of the World-Wide Church*
159. *The Book of Offices* (Methodist Church)
160. Revelation 1 : 5–6
161. B.C.P.
162. *New Every Morning*
163. *The Splendour of God* (Longmans, Green)
164. Oxford Mission to Calcutta (adapted)
165. Based on I Thessalonians 5
166. Abbot Marmion
167. Gilbert Shaw
168. W. O. Fitch, S.S.J.E.
169. *Prayers of the World-Wide Church*
170. R. M. Benson, S.S.J.E.
171. *Cuddesdon Office Book*
172. Ignatius Loyola (1491–1556)
173. Psalm 23.
174. B.C.P.
175. *New Every Morning*
176. Bishop George Bell
177. Sarum Breviary
178. F. B. Macnutt, *The Prayer Manual*
179. Based on words of Archbishop Michael Ramsey
180. G.A.
181. Revelation 5 : 9–10
182. The Rev. J. R. G. Ragg
183. *A Treasury of Prayers for Use in Toc H* (Toc H)
184. Source untraced
185. Quoted in *Prayers in Time of War* (S.C.M. Press)
186. Source untraced
187. G.A.
188. Psalm 22 : 27–28
189. *After the Third Collect*
190. *New Every Morning*
191. *The Kingdom, the Power and the Glory*
192. Harold Anson. *New Every Morning*
193. Based on Ephesians 3 : 14–15
194. *New Every Morning*
195. G.A.
196. *New Every Morning*

197. G.A.
198. Dean Vaughan. *Daily Prayer*
199. *After the Third Collect*
200. *Daily Prayer*
201. Philippians 4 : 7
202. Gregorian Sacramentary A.D. 590
203. G.A.
204. Bishop Pakenham Walsh
205. Psalm 67
206. G.A.
207. Quoted in *Truth and Dialogue* (edited by John Hick)
208. G. B. Molefe. *The World at One in Prayer*
209. John Mackenzie. *The World at One in Prayer*
210. G.A.
211. G.A.
212. G.A.
213. G.A.
214. G.A.
215. G.A.
216. G.A.
217. G.A.
218. Iknaton. *Hymn to the Sun* (14th century B.C.)
219. Quoted in G. Appleton, *Glad Encounter* (E.H.P.)
220. Quoted in G. Appleton, *Glad Encounter* (E.H.P.)
221. Quoted in *God of a Hundred Names*
222. Quoted from Trilochan Singh, *Songs of Nirvana* (Delhi)
223. Rabi'ah, died 801
224. Quoted in John Mbiti, *The Prayers of African Religion* (S.P.C.K.)
225. *B.C.P.*
226. Alcuin. *Daily Prayer*
227. Charles Kingsley. *Daily Prayer*
228. G.A.
229. G. W. Briggs. *The Prayer Manual*
230. Percy Dearmer
231. *B.C.P.*
232. *Acts of Devotion*
233. Leonine Sacramentary, trs.

Dean Armitage Robinson (450 A.D.)
234. *A Book of Prayers for Schools*
235. *A Procession of Passion Prayers*
236. Little Brothers of St. Francis
237. G.A.
238. S. C. Leung at I.M.C. Conference, Willingen 1952
239. Matthew 5 : 11–12 R.V.
240. *A Devotional Diary*
241. G.A.
242. *A Devotional Diary*
243. G.A.
244. *My God My Glory*
245. Based on Ephesians 3 : 14–19
246. Based on Philippians 1 : 9–11
247. I Samuel 12 : 23
248. *Daily Prayer*
249. G.A.
250. I Chronicles 29 : 11, 14
251. Oxford Mission to Calcutta
252. W. Bright, *Ancient Collects*
253. G.A.
254. *The Book of Common Order*
255. G.A.
256. Revelation 7 : 12
257. Gelasian Sacramentary, *c.* 500 A.D.
258. *My God My Glory*
259. G.A.
260. I Thessalonians 5 : 23 R.V.
261. *B.C.P.*
262. Church Missionary Society
263. Romans 15 : 5–6
264. E. Milner-White *Cambridge Bede Book* (Longmans, Green)
265. Bishop Westcott
266. *The World at One in Prayer*
267. Colossians 3 : 17
268. G.A.
269. Untraced
270. G.A.
271. *A Book of Prayers for Schools*
272. *Daily Prayer*
273. *The Kingdom, the Power and the Glory*
274. G.A.
275. G.A.

276. Quoted in H. M. Enomiya-Lassalle, *Zen: Way to Enlightenment* (Sheed & Ward)
277. G.A.
278. Henry VI. *Daily Prayer*
279. Rabi'ah, *c.* A.D. 900

280. *B.C.P.*
281. Based on words of Archbishop Temple
282. Psalm 150 : 1, 2, 6
283. Archbishop Goodier in *The Life that is Light* (adapted)

INDEX OF SUBJECTS

Those requiring prayers on special subjects will find considerable help in studying the table of contents on pages x–xii. More detailed information may be found in this index. The numbers given are those prefixed to the prayers; for the unnumbered biddings, thanksgivings and meditations page references are included.

INDEX OF BIBLE PASSAGES

206